Also from Quippery

FUR & PURR
THE FUNNIEST THINGS PEOPLE HAVE SAID ABOUT
CATS

FUR & GRRR

THE FUNNIEST THINGS PEOPLE HAVE SAID ABOUT

DOGS

Created by
Craig and Erich Pearson

A  BOOK

The Funniest Things People Have Said

Quippery LLC
Fairfield, Iowa 52557 USA

ISBN 978-1-949571-00-4

© Copyright 2018 by Quippery LLC

Published in the United States by Quippery LLC

Since this page cannot accommodate all the copyright notices, the copyright notices appear at the end of the book.

Cover design by George Foster, www.fostercovers.com

Printed with chlorine-free ink, on acid-free paper supplied by a Forest Stewardship Council certified supplier.

www.quippery.com

FUR & GRRR

CONTENTS

PROLOGUE

OUR QUEST FOR THE FUNNIEST THINGS PEOPLE HAVE SAID

THE RIVER

It was the only occasion when we had the faintest doubt about the wisdom of our quest.

We were in Brazil, canoeing up the Amazon River. We'd been there for the better part of a year.

The Amazon is 4,000 miles long — just 100 miles shorter than the world's longest river, the Nile. We'd passed through webs of ecosystems, with more biodiversity than any other region in the world. We wouldn't have been surprised to see a dinosaur wander out of the trees — in fact, some sections of the Amazon rainforest have remained intact since the dinosaur era. Because of all the carbon dioxide it absorbs and oxygen it produces, the Amazon rainforest is known as the *lungs of the earth*.

We paddled up a narrow tributary, the water quite still. We spotted a group of about twenty-five hyacinth macaws, the gorgeous blue parrots native to the region. They were huge, more than three feet tall, the world's largest parrots. Perched on branches, they watched us go by, turning their heads as we passed.

It was around noon when, suddenly, the placid water seemed to rise into a liquid arrow. A massive, long thing powered toward us. An anaconda — the world's biggest snake. This one was nearly 20 feet long, longer than our boat, more than 500 pounds of muscle.

With anacondas, it's not the bite you worry about — they don't have venom. They coil themselves around you and squeeze.

Anacondas, we'd been told, can hunt on land, taking down deer, jaguars, antelopes. But they prefer hunting in the water.

This one, olive green, was coming straight at us, eyes high on its head, its rippling muscular back shining wet in the sunlight.

The anaconda hit our boat straight on, hurtling us into the water.

To our astonishment, the massive snake kept on going — where, we couldn't tell.

Our relief was only momentary.

"Didn't they tell us in the last village that there are piranhas in this river?" one of us asked.

"They did. They stressed sharp teeth and powerful jaws."

"And told us how, when one of their goats slipped into the water, it was gone in a minute."

We lost no time clambering toward shore, sensitive to whether flesh was being removed from our skeletons. Up the bank we crawled, canoe in tow, warm river water falling from our bodies.

We looked each other up and down. All musculature seemed intact.

"Brother," one of us said, at length. "Is this really worth it?"

"Please don't go there," the other replied.

"No, seriously — it's a noble quest and everything. But is it worth *dying* for?"

The river gleamed in the morning sunlight. Hyacinth macaws cawed from upstream.

We turned the canoe upside down and emptied the water. Setting it back on the river, we climbed in and resumed paddling — continuing our life quest for the funniest things people have said.

Look for more adventure tales in each Quippery book.

IN THE BEGINNING

On the origin of dogs and cats

And Adam said, "Lord, when we were in the garden, you walked with us every day. Now we do not see you anymore. We are lonesome here, and it is difficult for us to remember how much you love us."

And God said, "Child, I will create a companion for you that will be with you and who will be a reflection of my love for you, so that you will love me even when you cannot see me. Regardless of how selfish or childish or unlovable you may be, this new companion will accept you as you are and will love you as I do, in spite of yourselves."

And God created a new animal to be a companion for them. And it was a good animal. And God was pleased. And the new animal was pleased to be with Adam and Eve and wagged its tail.

And Adam said, "But Lord, I have already named all the animals in the Kingdom and I cannot think of a name for this new animal."

And God said, "As I have created this new animal to be a reflection of my love for you, his name will be a reflection of my own name, and you will call him DOG."

And Dog lived with Adam and Eve and was a companion to them and loved them. And they were comforted. And God was pleased.

And Dog was content and wagged its tail in appreciation of its beloved masters.

It came to pass that an angel went to the Lord and said, "Lord, Adam and Eve have become filled with pride. They strut and preen like peacocks and they believe they are worthy of adoration. Dog has indeed taught them that they are loved, but perhaps too well."

And God said, "Verily, I will create for them a companion who will be with them and who will see them as they are. The companion will remind them of their limitations, so they will know that they are not worthy of adoration."

And God created CAT to be a companion to Adam and Eve. And Cat would not obey them. And when they gazed into Cat's eyes, they were reminded that they were not supreme beings.

And Adam and Eve learned humility.

And they were greatly improved. And God was pleased and Dog was happy.

And Cat didn't give a damn one way or the other.

— Unknown

Where do dogs *really* come from?

Think of your poodle's parents — or your Golden's, your Labrador's, or whatever you've got. And then their parents . . . and their parents . . . and their parents.

Ultimately — billions of sets of parents into the past — you come to your dog's Adam and Eve. They were even smaller than teacup poodles — a few hundred thousand of them could fit inside the period at the end of this sentence. They were the bacteria and other single-celled creatures that floated in the oceans a few billion years ago.

Teensy though they were, you could still tell they were dogs' ancestors — each one had a wagging tail (technically, a *flagellum*). They were always happy to see each other, and since there were quintillions of them in every neighborhood, they had a lot to be happy about. So lots of tail wagging.

These dog ancestors pioneered what later became today's dog shows. There were no flying disc catches, no weave races through poles and barrels, no high jumping feats — such athletic dog feats would develop some years later, after these creatures became larger, moved onto land, grew legs and fur, and found owners. In the original bacteria shows, the main tricks consisted of swaying in the water, wagging their teeny flagella, absorbing food, and dividing themselves in two. This last trick was always great fun for everyone. In the space of ten hours, one of them could become a billion of them.

Judges had a hard time telling them apart, especially when trillions competed at a time and judges could see them only through microscopes. So every bacterium that showed up got a prize.

Today's dogs, unfortunately, have forgotten the ancient art of rapidly dividing in two. That would have been a big hit in modern dog shows.

— Robert Wilde

God sat down for a moment when the dog was finished in order to watch it . . . and to know that it was good, that nothing was lacking, that it could not have been made better.

— Rainer Maria Rilke

To Dog, Or Not To Dog:
That is the Question

Why not? Just about everyone else has one. There are 90 million dogs in US households today, and the number is rising. That's one for every 3.6 people, which means we have a lot of 0.6 people in this country.

Add these 90 million dogs to the 326 million people in America, and the total comes to 416 million. This means the 90 million dogs make up nearly 22% of our people-dog population. This doesn't count the tens of millions of stray dogs, no doubt working for lower wages.

Aware of their growing strength, dogs are now campaigning for the right to vote and starting to unionize. They're also petitioning for single-payer health care, longer vacations, paid maternity leave, etc. If all the European dogs have these things, they argue, why can't American dogs?

Keep all this in mind as you consider whether to get a dog.

If you do get a dog, please share it with a 0.6 person. Those people have a hard time getting any dog's attention.

My husband and I are either going to buy a dog or have a child. We can't decide whether to ruin our carpet or ruin our lives.

— Rita Rudner

Every boy should have two things: a dog, and a mother willing to let him have one.

— Unknown

Every boy who has a dog should also have a mother, so the dog can be fed regularly.

— Unknown

I was thinking of getting a German Shepherd once, but I didn't want to learn another language just to have a dog.

— Unknown

from Dave Barry

Have you ever wondered why people have pets? Neither have I. I suspect it's because pets are easy to talk to. I spend hours talking to my dog, explaining my views on world affairs. She always listens very attentively, although I'm not sure she understands me. If I could hear what she's thinking, it would probably go like this:

ME: The situation in the Middle East certainly looks serious.

MY DOG: I wonder if he's going to give me some food.

ME: It is unfortunate that an area so vital to the economic well-being of the world is so politically unstable.

MY DOG: Maybe he'll give me some food now.

ME: The Russians certainly are making it difficult for our government to achieve a lasting Mideast peace.

MY DOG: Any minute now he might go into the kitchen and get me some food.

— *Dave Barry's Bad Habits*

from The New Yorker

Pets Immediately Available for Adoption

Jason Roeder

Thank you for your interest in adopting a pet! While we can't guarantee that every dog or cat you see listed on our Web site will be available at the shelter when you arrive, there are several members of our furry family that have been with us quite a while and will almost certainly be here, eagerly awaiting you. Help give them the love they desperately, *desperately* need!

Jake

This three-year-old boxer mix suffered years of psychological abuse at the hands of his prior owners, in Brooklyn, who named him Terrence Q. Fluffernutter, Esq., for no discernible reason. Though he is slowly adjusting to having a real dog's name, Jake remains understandably skittish and could benefit from a less traumatically ironic environment.

Wanda

It's a mystery to us why this six-year-old calico has been here so long, other than the fact that she sits perfectly still all day — like, totally motionless. Never moves. This kitty would be perfect for any home that's looking for a low-maintenance pet or is seriously considering adopting a small pile of leaves.

Rufus

This terrier's face was badly wounded in a fight with a raccoon, but the disfigurement hasn't stopped anyone here from getting in lots of snuggles with him, provided that he is wearing the special balaclava that allows him to breathe but covers all exposed skin and bone. Rufus is best suited for a home that understands one simple rule: The special balaclava does not come off. The balaclava never comes off.

Coco

Here's one cocker spaniel that's great with kids — and only kids! While aggressive around adults, Coco would make a great companion for runaways or just children left at home unsupervised for weeks at a time.

Pepper

Somebody needs a tummy rub! But that somebody is not Pepper. A purrfect addition to any family, this five-year-old domestic shorthair is a cuddle machine! Except for his belly. Even approach his fluffy white tum-tum, and he'll recoil and fix his eyes on you as if to say, "How dare you? Is there any trace of compassion inside you? Dostoevsky said that no animal could be as cruel as a man, and here you are, living testament to his word. You are the surest sign that if, *if,* God exists, he weeps for having made you in his image and for making me your mere toy."

Chloe

We will straight-up pay you five hundred dollars if you make Chloe disappear.

Boots

What if a cat was trained for dog-fighting but was subsequently forced into retirement because her bloodlust disturbed even her trainer? Come on down and meet Boots! We found this gray tabby gnawing straight through a tire three days ago. In the short time since then, every single one of us at the shelter has grown to fear and respect her! Boots probably isn't the best fit for a home with children in it — even visiting ones, even just in your doorway, trick-or-treating — and would be happiest in . . . we actually shudder to think what would make Boots happy. It may be best if the world never knows.

The dog is a yes-animal. Very popular with people who can't afford a yes man.

— Robertson Davies

from The Onion

Choosing The Right Dog For You

Once you decide to get a dog, there's a wide range of adoptable pets to choose from, whether it's a mutt or purebred. The Onion offers some helpful tips for choosing the dog that's right for you.

- First, decide which type of dog hair you want to stick to everything you own for the rest of your life.

- Find a reputable breeder who is certified by the American Kennel Club and truly cares about the purity of the canine master race.

- Do some research into which breeds have the highest resale value.

- A collie is a great choice for families with particularly dim-witted kids who keep falling down holes.

- Many shelter dogs have abandonment issues, so don't get one of those.

- If you're looking to get a dog, be sure to check the classifieds.

The ideal age for a boy to own a dog is between forty-five and fifty.

— Robert Benchley

Classified dog ads

FOUND DIRTY WHITE DOG: Looks like a rat, been out a while. Better be a reward.

FREE YORKSHIRE TERRIER: 8 years old. Hateful little dog. Bites.

FREE PUPPIES: Part German Shepherd, part stupid dog.

FREE GERMAN SHEPHERD: 85 lbs. Neutered. Speaks German.

FREE PUPPIES: Half cocker spaniel, half sneaky neighbor's dog.

SINGLE BLACK FEMALE seeks male companionship, ethnicity unimportant. I'm a very good-looking girl who LOVES to play. I love long walks in the woods, riding in your pickup truck, hunting, camping and fishing trips, cozy winter nights lying by the fire. Candlelight dinners will have me eating out of your hand. Rub me the right way and watch me respond. I'll be at the front door when you get home from work, wearing only what nature gave me. Kiss me and I'm yours. Call . . . and ask for Daisy.

— Ad in a city newspaper. Hundreds of men found themselves talking to the city's Humane Society about an 8-week-old black Labrador Retriever.

from Merrill Markoe

When my dog Stan died, there were a couple of weeks when I lived pet-free. I fantasized that finally not being tied down to a dependent would give my spontaneous nature a chance to grow and flower. Then I realized that not only didn't I have much of a spontaneous nature but that the reason I wasn't partaking of the constant barrage of interesting activities and social events all around me was because I was a lazy sloth. Eventually this caused me to see myself in such an unflattering light that I had no choice but to go straight to the pound and come home with a puppy. And since that time, I have never had to look my own inadequacies squarely in the eye again because I have been blessed by the constant inconveniences of pet ownership.

— *How to be Hap Hap Happy Like Me*

When your children are teenagers, it's important to have a dog so that someone in the house is happy to see you.

— Nora Ephron, *I Feel Bad About My Neck*

If you want to be liked, get a dog. The people you work with are not your friends.

— Deborah Norville

If you want sex, have an affair. If you want a relationship, buy a dog.

— Julia Burchill

DO YOU HAVE WHAT IT TAKES TO OWN A DOG?
(DOES A DOG HAVE WHAT IT TAKES TO BE YOUR PET?)

Mixed-Breed Aptitude Tests (MBAT) for Dog Owners and Dogs

Since many of us have been schooled to believe that only by taking tests can we really come to know our proclivities and aptitudes, we offer you the security of that all-American standby, the multiple-choice aptitude test.

In fact, we offer you two — one for you as a prospective owner and one for your dog, since it is unrealistic to overlook the fact that although you may think you have selected the right dog, the dog may not share your enthusiasm.

A special grading pencil is not needed to take the test — any old Mongol will do. Circle the appropriate letter for each question.

THE MBAT FOR DOG OWNERS

1. If a strange dog barks at you, do you:

    a. Make an obscene gesture at him

    b. Go after him with a stick

    c. Run away in fright

    d. Bark back until he shuts up

    e. Reassure the dog in a friendly tone that you mean no harm and walk away slowly

2. If you felt like a bit of exercise, would you:

    a. Promise yourself to do some sit-ups tomorrow

    b. Run over to the television and turn on the football game

    c. Take a walk in the park and leave the dog at home

    d. Walk the dog down to the corner for a six-pack and walk back home to watch the football game

    e. Take the dog on your daily two-mile jog

3. If your dog made a "mistake" on the living room rug, would you:

    a. Throw a newspaper on top of it and walk around it

b. Erect a run in the living room, figuring if that's where he's going to go, that's where he's going to go

c. Tell him to get out and never come back

d. Rub his nose in it and hit him with a newspaper

e. Say "no" firmly, take him outside for five minutes, and keep alert the next time the dog is in the living room

4. If you had to shop for dog food, would you:

a. Let the dog shop for his own food

b. Not shop at all but feed him leftovers and tell him to think of all the starving Armenians

c. Buy the most expensive, most heavily advertised food on the market

d. Read the ingredients on the label, compare them to a canine nutritional requirement chart, and conduct a personal taste survey

5. If you found out that you couldn't keep your dog because of an allergy, would you:

a. Ask the vet to put him to sleep

b. Let him go, hoping that someone nice will find him

    c. Give him to your mother, because she's such a soft touch

    d. Move out of the house and let the dog stay

    e. Do everything you can to find him a good home, calling the local humane shelter as the last resort

6. If your dog bit a neighborhood child, would you:

    a. Beat the kid for being a pest

    b. Bite the dog to let him know what it feels like

    c. Blame the neighbors for the accident, charging that the child led the dog on, and threaten to sue for abuse

    d. Introduce the dog to a dog trainer

    e. Inform the child's parents and keep the dog confined, under observation for two weeks for signs of rabies

7. If your dog looked unkempt and dirty, would you:

    a. Ignore it, 'cause that's how dogs are

    b. Tell him not to come home until he looked more presentable

    c. Run him under the hose a couple of times as he runs through the yard

    d. Take him to Vidal Sassoon

e. Give him a good brushing, and if he's still dirty, bathe and dry him thoroughly

8. If your female dog got out while in heat and had a whirl with the locals, would you:

a. Buy a box of cigars

b. Wonder why your wife isn't as willing as your dog

c. Slap a paternity suit on the owner of the winning dog

d. Let the dog have her pups and give them to the kids to unload at school

e. Let the dog have her pups, find each of them a good home, and have her spayed

9. If your dog always jumped up on people, would you:

a. Tell them they were lucky the dog hadn't bitten them

b. Take a "dogs-will-be-dogs" attitude

c. Hit him on the head until he gets down

d. Enroll him in obedience school

e. Spend ten minutes a day teaching him not to jump up and discipline him firmly whenever he does

10. If you went away for a vacation, would you:

    a. Leave the dog at home with an open, ten-pound bag of dog kibble

    b. Tell the dog to sponge off the neighbors for a couple of weeks

    c. Leave the dog home and have one of the neighborhood kids check on him every couple of days

    d. Inspect several kennels recommended by your veterinarian and choose the cleanest and most effectively run

    e. Find a vacation retreat that allows pets and take the dog with you

Count your points: $a = 1$, $b = 2$, $c = 3$, $d = 4$, and $e = 5$.

YOUR SCORE:

• **Between 40 and 50** — You are a dog owner's dog owner and need no further coaching whatsoever.

• **Between 30 and 40** — You have the potential for being a satisfactory dog owner, but you need to read this book.

• **Between 20 and 30** — You're a schizophrenic type, but a few years of psychoanalysis and a thorough reading of every dog manual you can get your hands on might bring you around.

• **Between 10 and 20** — Get a cat.

Less than 10 — you can't cope with yourself. Your best bet would be to get a dog to take care of you.

THE MBAT FOR DOGS

1. If you saw a slipper, would your instinct be to:

   a. Eat it

   b. Bury it

   c. Check to see if it's your size

   d. Look at the label to see if it came from Gucci and then check to see if it's your size

   e. Take it to your owner when he/she gets home from work

2. If an intruder entered your home, would you:

   a. Smile

   b. Bite his ankle

   c. Offer him a drink

   d. Sniff to see if he's clean

   e. Bark ferociously and hope that he goes away

3. If you went into the kitchen and found a piece of roast beef sitting unattended on the counter, would you:

    a. Eat it on the spot and bury the bone

    b. Lick it all over and leave the room

    c. Check to see if it's medium rare before eating it

    d. Ignore it because of its high cholesterol

    e. Put it in the refrigerator so it won't go bad

4. If you saw a loose puppy wandering down the street, would you:

    a. Chase him into the street in front of a car to teach him a lesson he'll never forget

    b. Chase him into a neighbor's yard and beat him up in front of a bunch of kids

    c. Check his tag before taking action to make sure his name is not too ethnic

    d. Ask him what country club his owners belong to

    e. Chase him home and stay there until his owner promises not to let it happen again

5. In the veterinarian's office, would you:

   a) Shake uncontrollably, feign timidity, and bite the vet when he gets you on the table

   b) Whine during the examination and scream bloody murder when you get your injection

   c) Seduce the cute little bitch next to you

   d) Insist that the vet scrub down the examination table twice before placing you on it

   e) Remain calm and quiet, refusing to leave until the vet remembers that you also need a heartworm test

6. When you relieve yourself, do you:

   a. Aim for someone's leg

   b. Scratch at the screen door until you make a hole that you can jump through

   c. Find a little-used corner of the house and take care of things quietly

   d. Refuse to go at all until the bathroom has been wiped down with Lysol

   e. Aim for a tree growing in soil deficient in uric acid

7. If you were given a doggie toy, would you:

    a. Chew it to bits instantly

    b. Ignore it because you'd rather have something else — like a steak

    c. Check the price to see if it's worth wasting your time on

    d. Thank the donor very much but allow as how you've really outgrown that kind of stuff

    e. Play with it energetically for fifteen minutes, then put it away in your toy box

8. After you have played in a muddy area, do you:

    a. Go into the house and shake the dirt all over the place

    b. Go into the front hall and roll on the rug to avoid carrying mud throughout the house

    c. Go into the house and jump on your owner's bed

    d. Refuse to come in until you have been bathed and dried

    e. None of the above — you wouldn't be caught dead in mud

9. If you knew that it was suppertime and nothing seemed to be happening, would you:

    a. Open the refrigerator and help yourself

    b. Go next door and raid the garbage cans

    c. Ring for room service

    d. Write an irate letter to the management

    e. Wait patiently, remembering that your time is your owner's time

10. When your owner takes you for a walk, do you:

    a. Pull like crazy on your leash so that your owner has to hang on with all his might

    b. Bite him when he tries to put a leash on you

    c. Make him follow three steps behind you

    d. Make him wear the leash

    e. Walk (or trot) at his left side, keeping exactly abreast and in step

Count your points: $a = 1$, $b = 2$, $c = 3$, $d = 4$, and $e = 5$.

YOUR SCORE:

• **Over 50** — You're not as smart as you think you are — there are only 50 possible points.

• **Between 40 and 50** — You are an incredibly well-behaved and thoughtful animal and should probably be an owner, not an ownee.

• **Between 30 and 40** — You are quite fastidious and genteel, and care a great deal about the niceties of life. You will need to invoke a great deal of discretion when choosing an owner, because there are many around who will not understand you or appreciate your discriminating characteristics.

• **Between 20 and 30** — You have a very great sense of self and like to have things your own way. You, too, may have a problem finding the right owner. Remember, an owner, by his very nature, likes to have the upper hand.

• **Between 10 and 20** — Your canine instincts are strong and you could use a little help in the obedience department and are somewhat impervious to humans, but you're probably not going to have trouble finding an owner.

• **10 or below** — You're a real dog.

— Unknown

DOGS VS. CATS

It's the topic of endless debate: Dogs or cats? Which makes the better pet?

If you count how people vote with their feet — or rather their pets — cats edge out dogs. The count is 95.6 million pet cats to 90 million pet dogs in the US. (Bear in mind this is only the popular vote — we're still awaiting the Electoral College results.)

Any dog owners care to demand a recount?

The only thing better than the world's cutest cat is any dog.

— Daniel Tosh

Every dog has his day — but the nights are reserved for cats.

— Unknown

The cat is mightily dignified until the dog comes along.

— Unknown

I got my dog three years ago because I was drunk in a pet store. We had nine cats at the time. The cats started hiding the alcohol after that.

— Paula Poundstone

I put contact lenses in my dog's eyes. They had little pictures of cats on them. Then I took one out and he ran around in circles.

— Steven Wright

A dog accepts you as the boss. A cat wants to see your resume.

— Unknown

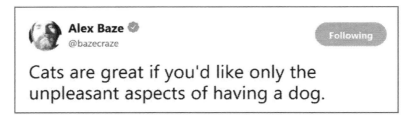

If a dog jumps into your lap, it is because he is fond of you; but if a cat does the same thing, it is because your lap is warmer.

— Alfred North Whitehead

Women and cats will do as they please, and men and dogs should relax and get used to the idea.

— Robert A. Heinlein

If animals could speak, the dog would be a blundering outspoken fellow; but the cat would have the rare grace of never saying a word too much.

— Mark Twain

Adopt a dog? Or a cat?

- If you want someone who will eat whatever you put in front of him and never say it's not as good as his mother's . . . then adopt a dog.

- If you want someone always willing to go out with you, at any hour, for as long and wherever you want . . . then adopt a dog.

- If you want someone who will never touch the remote, doesn't care about football, and can sit next to you as you watch romantic movies . . . then adopt a dog.

- If you want someone who is content to get on your bed just to warm your feet and whom you can push off if he snores . . . then adopt a dog.

- If you want someone who never criticizes what you do, doesn't care if you are pretty or ugly, fat or thin, young or old, who acts as if every word you say is especially worthy of his attention, and loves you unconditionally, perpetually . . . then adopt a dog.

- On the other hand, if you want someone who never responds when you call, ignores you when you come home, walks all over you, runs around all night and comes home only to eat and sleep, and acts as if your entire existence is solely to ensure his happiness . . . then adopt a cat.

— Unknown

Dogs would make totally incompetent criminals. If you could somehow get a group of dogs to understand the concept of the Kennedy assassination, they would all immediately confess to it. Whereas you'll never see a cat display any kind of guilty behavior, despite the fact that several cats were seen in Dallas on the grassy knoll area, not that I wish to start rumors.

— Dave Barry

Why dogs are better than cats

- Dogs will tilt their heads and try to understand every word you say. Cats will ignore you and take a nap.

- Cats look silly on a leash.

- When you come home from work, your dog will be happy and lick your face. Cats will still be mad at you for leaving in the first place.

- Dogs will give you unconditional love until the day they die. Cats will make you pay for every mistake you've ever made since the day you were born.

- A dog knows when you're sad. And he'll try to comfort you. Cats don't care how you feel, as long as you remember where the can opener is.

- Dogs will bring you your slippers. Cats will drop a dead mouse in your slippers.

- When you take them for a ride, dogs will sit on the seat next to you. Cats need their own private basket, or they won't go at all.

- Dogs will play fetch with you all day long. The only thing cats will play with all day long are small rodents or bugs, preferably ones that look like they're in pain.

- Dogs will wake you up if the house is on fire. Cats will quietly sneak out the back door.

— Unknown

A dog thinks . . .

Hey, those people I live with feed me, love me, provide me with a nice warm, dry house, pet me, and take good care of me. . . . *They must be gods!*

A cat thinks . . .

Hey, those people I live with feed me, love me, provide me with a nice warm, dry house, pet me, and take good care of me. . . . *I must be a god!*

Why cats are better than dogs

- Cats purr. Dogs drool.

- Cats rub your leg when they want affection, not when they're horny.

- Cats use a litter box. Dogs use your leg.

- In 1996, over 10,000 US deaths were attributed to a dog owner's choking on saliva during morning wake-up licks.

- Cats always land on their feet. Dogs just won't let you throw them.

- Cats will wait until you've read your morning paper before tearing it to shreds.

- Cats look cute sleeping on the TV. Dogs just crash right in front of the screen.

- Fewer cat owners suffer from "Flappy Tail" lacerations than dog owners.

- No one has ever had to "Beware of the Cat."

- Cats bury their crap. Dogs dig up others'.

- Cats have better things to do than stick their nose in your crotch.

- Cats lay themselves on the car in the heat. Dogs in heat lay the car.

- Why do you think they call it *dog breath?*

- Garfield. Odie. Enough said.

— Unknown

The cat's motto

No matter what you've done wrong, always try to make it look like the dog did it.

— Unknown

You own a dog but you feed a cat.

— Jenny de Vries

If you can look at a dog and not feel vicarious excitement and affection, you must be a cat.

— Unknown

The truth about dogs and cats

WHAT IS A DOG?

- Dogs lie around all day, sprawled on the most comfortable piece of furniture in the house.

- They can hear a package of food opening half a block away, but don't hear you when you're in the same room.

- They can look dumb and lovable all at the same time.

- They growl when they are not happy.

- When you want to play, they want to play.

- When you want to be alone, they want to play.

- They are great at begging.

- They will love you forever if you rub their tummies.

- They can never have enough toys and they leave them everywhere.

- They do disgusting things with their mouths and then they try to give you a kiss.

CONCLUSION – *Dogs are tiny little men in fur coats.*

WHAT IS A CAT?

- Cats do what they want.

- They rarely listen to you.

- They're totally unpredictable.

- They whine when they are not happy.

- When you want to play, they want to be alone.

- When you want to be alone, they want to play.

- They expect you to cater to their every whim.

- They're moody.

- They leave hair everywhere.

- They drive you nuts and cost you money.

CONCLUSION – *Cats are tiny little women in fur coats.*

— Unknown

Cats will outsmart dogs every time.

— John Grogan

Dogs believe they are human. Cats believe they are God.

— Jeff Valdez

Dogs eat. Cats dine.

— Ann Taylor

Dogs come when they're called. Cats take a message and get back to you later.

— Mary Bly

You call to a dog and a dog will break its neck to get to you. Dogs just want to please. Call to a cat and its attitude is, "What's in it for me?"

— Lewis Grizzard

The dog may be wonderful prose, but only the cat is poetry.

— French proverb

Dogs look up to you. Cats look down on you. Give me a pig. He just looks you in the eye and treats you like an equal.

— Sir Winston Churchill

Dogs seem more photogenic than cats. In photos most cats look like sociopaths.

— Demetri Martin

from Dave Barry

How To Deal With Subordinates

Remember the old saying: "A subordinate capable of thinking up an idea is a subordinate capable of realizing that there is no particular reason why he or she should be a subordinate, especially your subordinate." This is why dogs are so popular as pets. You can have a dog for its whole lifetime, and it will never once come up with a good idea. It will lie around for over a decade, licking its private parts and always reacting with total wonder and amazement to your ideas. "What!?" says the dog, when you call it to the door. "You want me to go *outside*!!? What a *great* idea!!! I never would have thought of that!!!"

Cats, on the other hand, don't think you're the least bit superior. They're always watching you with that smartass cat expression and thinking, "God, what a cementhead." Cats are always coming up with their own ideas. They are not team players, and they would make terrible corporate employees. A corporate department staffed by cats would be a real disciplinary nightmare, the kind of department that would never achieve 100 percent of its "fair share" pledge quota to the United Way. Dogs, on the other hand, would go way over the quota. Of course they'd also chew up the pledge cards.

The point I'm trying to make here, as far as I can tell, is that you want subordinates who, when it comes to thinking up ideas, are more like dogs than like cats.

— *Claw Your Way to the Top*

When dogs leap onto your bed, it's because they adore being with you. When cats leap onto your bed, it's because they adore your bed.

— Alisha Everett

Cats are the ultimate narcissists. You can tell this because of all the time they spend on personal grooming. Dogs aren't like this. A dog's idea of personal grooming is to roll on a dead fish.

— James Gorman

The dog is mentioned in the Bible eighteen times — the cat not even once.

— W.E. Farbstein

The bottom line: Get *something!*

A house without either a cat or a dog is the house of a scoundrel.

— Portuguese proverb

NAME DAT DOG

You might be a redneck if your dog's name is Miller Light.

— Jeff Foxworthy

I bought a dog the other day. I named him Stay. It's fun to call him, "Come here, Stay! Come here, Stay!" He went insane. Now he just ignores me and keeps typing.

— Steven Wright

They say that you can tell man apart from other animals by his ability to reason. I think you could also go by last names. What's his name? Patches? Patches what? That's a dog. Don't waste my time.

— Demetri Martin

Suitable for naming

You could give your dog an ordinary name like Max, Charlie, Cooper, Buddy, or Jack, or Bella, Lucy, Daisy, Luna, and Lola — the actual top five names for male and female dogs from a recent survey.

But do you want to follow the masses? Or chose a mode not taken?

We'd have been proud to have created these names — familiar names twisted into handles suitable for extraordinary dogs:

- Bark Twain
- Chewbarka
- Droolius Caesar
- Franz Furrdinand
- Fyodor Dogstoevsky
- Hairy Pawter
- Jimmy Chew
- Kareem Abdul JaBark
- Mary Puppins
- Orville Redenbarker
- Prince of Barkness
- Salvador Dogi
- Sherlock Bones

- Winnie the Poodle
- Woofgang Puck
- Groucho Barks
- Lady Dogiva
- Dumbledog
- Queen of Barkness
- Sir Licks A Lot
- Pup Tart
- Muttley Crue
- Indiana Bones
- The Dogfather

keith
@KeetPotato

Following

wife: "no"
me: "its a good name"
wife: "keith we're not calling the dog sarah jessica barker, keep thinking"
me:
wife:
me: "woofie goldberg"

PUPPY LOVE

Question to ponder: Are puppies as cute and irresistible as kittens?

  If you're a dog owner, let your cat owner friends know what you think. And vice versa.

The best way to get a puppy is to beg for a baby brother — and they'll settle for a puppy every time.

— Winston Pendleton

There is no psychiatrist in the world like a puppy licking your face.

— Ben Williams

I just got another puppy. I now have two. I didn't want another one, but I got her when my nieces were visiting. I thought we'd kill a couple hours at the pet store. There was a little girl puppy that looks like my puppy and the kids were playing with her. It's time to go, and I'm zipping up the three-year-old's coat and she's crying. I asked, "What's the matter, Julianna?" "Inside my heart I'm very much hurting, because we're leaving her in the cage and it looks like a jail and she didn't do anything wrong, and I'm so sorry we're not going to keep her, because I love you more than I love Mommy and Daddy." *Wrap it up.*

— Unknown

Whoever said you can't buy happiness forgot about puppies.

— Gene Hill

A puppy plays with every pup he meets, but an old dog has few associates.

— Josh Billings

RAISING CANINES

As soon as a dog enters your household, new mutual expectations and responsibilities take hold. These include providing food, training, morning walks outside, toys, medical care, and most of all, a loving, caring presence. And that's just what your *dog* is expected to provide *you*.

When you get a dog, you become a player in an industry approximately the size of the military-industrial complex. You'll want the best of everything the dog industry offers. Organic food. Organic vitamin and mineral supplements. Stress relievers. Hip and joint formulas. Dog grooming salons and dog spas. Dog umbrellas. Purses that match yours. Nail polish. Cologne. Necklaces. Beer. Painting kits. Wearable poop catchers. Butt covers. And more. (We're not inventing any of this.)

Wearables are essential. These enable your dogs to track your physical activity, location, and health metrics. (You can also get them for your dogs.)

You'll definitely want the Internet-connected video cameras and treat dispensers that enable your dogs to engage with you via Skype-like connections while you're away from home. Now they'll be able to bark and whine at you and demand you open the door no matter where you are. These smart devices aim to take the stress out of caring for your pet by making caring for your pet a 24/7 responsibility.

We have two dogs, Mabel and Wolf, and three cats at home, Charlie, George and Chairman. We have two cats on our farm, Tom and Little Sister, two horses, and two mini horses, Hannah and Tricky. We also have two cows, Holy and Madonna. And those are only the animals we let sleep in our bed.

— Ellen DeGeneres

Anybody who doesn't know what soap tastes like never washed a dog.

— Franklin P. Jones

from The New Yorker

A Bill for All Debts Accrued by My Dog

Susanna Wolff

Dear Valued Pet,

You have an outstanding balance on your account. An itemized list of billable goods and services is as follows:

25-lb. bag of organic, grain-free, mega-expensive dog food

25-lb. bag of different food because you decided you didn't like the fancy other food even though you've always gobbled it down like a monster in the past

1 of the best, most humane, pressure-point-free harnesses on the market

1 new, regular harness because I got sick of explaining to smug busybodies in the park that the humane harness just looked inhumane because you insisted on strangling yourself with it anyway

¼-lb. of Taleggio you ate off the coffee table during a dinner party

1 salami on which you tentatively placed your tongue before party guests arrived and that I served anyway

4-16 dog hairs in every single cup of coffee I've had since you came into my home

1 accidental "like" of a former classmate/current stranger's Birthright-trip Instagram when I tried to brush one of your hairs off my phone

62 weeks, that's how deep into that Instagram feed I was, just F.Y.I.

1 discovery that your hair wasn't just on my phone screen, but actually embedded under the glass

3 pairs of headphones eaten in their entirety

1 pair of headphones merely shredded beyond repair, which allowed me to figure out what happened to the other 3 pairs

1 lifetime's worth of feces picked up with only a flimsy Citarella produce bag protecting my hand

8 attempts at subtly studying said feces in public for any sign of those headphones

2 trips to the vet

45 minutes trying to get you to pee into a little plastic dish thing only to have the whole mess tip over onto my shoe

$624 to find out that you're fine

Another ¼-lb. of Taleggio, somehow

Total amount due: $6,346

Payment due: 4/24/2015

If payment is not received by 4/24/2015, I will have no choice but to keep providing for you and loving you anyway because you are my dog.

Thank you for allowing me to serve you.

Sincerely,

Your Indentured Owner

Susanna Wolff

Don't sweat the sweater stuff

If you are a dog and your owner suggests that you wear a sweater, suggest that he wear a tail.

— Fran Lebowitz

It's always the little dogs you see wearing sweaters. My neighbor's dog has a sweater, but he wears it just wrapped around his shoulders.

— Ellen DeGeneres

I saw a dog wearing a sweater and I thought that looked ridiculous because dogs don't have arms. If you're going to put clothes on the dog, you should put two pairs of pants on it.

— Demetri Martin

IT'S A DOG EAT DOG FOOD WORLD

The dog's kennel is not the place to keep a sausage.

— Danish proverb

Get a good dog. We have not picked up food in the kitchen in 15 years.

— Paul Reiser

from Dave Barry

You should choose a recipe that is appropriate for the individuals who will be eating it. For example, you do not need to make an elaborate dish if the individuals are dogs. A dog will eat pretty much anything; one major reason why there are no restaurants for dogs is that the customers would eat the menus. So a dog will happily eat the same recipe forever. You can feed a dog "kibble," which is actually compressed dirt, every single day for 13 years, and the dog will consider you to be the greatest cook in world history. It will lick the ground you walk on.

— *Dave Barry Is Not Taking This Sitting Down*

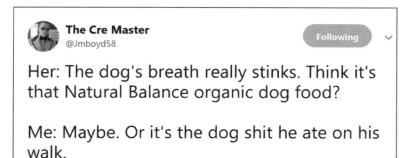

The Cre Master
@Jmboyd58

Following

Her: The dog's breath really stinks. Think it's that Natural Balance organic dog food?

Me: Maybe. Or it's the dog shit he ate on his walk.

I don't eat anything that a dog won't eat. Like sushi. Ever see a dog eat sushi? He just sniffs it and says, "I don't think so." And this is an animal that licks between its legs and sniffs fire hydrants.

— William Corone

My dog is worried about the economy because Alpo is up to 99 cents a can. That's almost $7.00 in dog money.

— Joe Weinstein

Compared to their sense of smell, dogs seem to pay a lot less attention to their sense of taste. Apparently they believe that if something fits into their mouths, then it is food, no matter what it tastes like.

— Stanley Coren

They have dog food for constipated dogs. If your dog is constipated, why screw up a good thing? Stay indoors and let 'em bloat!

— David Letterman

What a dog I got, his favorite bone is in my arm.

— Rodney Dangerfield

from Dave Barry

What kind of dog food is best for your dog?

What kind of dog food is best for your dog? Many dog owners have strong views on this subject, which is one way you can tell they are insane. The best food for your dog is: brown dog food. Oh, sure, you'll see TV ads claiming that a certain brand is superior, as evidenced by the fact that the dog in the commercial is enthusiastically chowing down on it. But what these ads fail to tell you is that the same dog would chow down, with equal enthusiasm, on any other brand of dog food, or any brand of cat food, or an actual cat, or a pair of soiled underpants, or the Declaration of Independence, or a clarinet.

Dogs did not get where they are today by being picky eaters. Back in prehistoric times, they were competing with the rest of their pack for food, and if they came across, say, the decaying carcass of a mastodon, they had to snatch whatever piece they could, because if they didn't, some other dog would. They'd swallow the piece quickly, and then, if it didn't agree with them, they'd simply throw it back up later, and some other dog would eat it. Or maybe the same dog would eat it again, because, as we have established, dogs are not the nuclear physicists of the animal kingdom. In this manner a pack of dogs could transport a single rancid mastodon rectum thousands of miles.

In modern times dogs still operate on the principle that you should eat first and worry later about whether what you ate was edible. My current dog, Lucy, eats, among many other things, photo albums. The first time she did this, we told her she was Bad, which made her feel very sorry and press herself into the floor like a big hairy remorseful worm. But a few days later she ate another photo album. Again she felt terribly guilty, but she obviously believed, in what passes for her mind, that she had no choice, because if she didn't eat the album, another dog might, and that was a chance she simply could not afford to take.

— *I'll Mature When I'm Dead*

Some scientist spent twenty years in the lab inventing ice cream for dogs. He made it taste like vanilla, so it's hardly selling at all. If he'd made it taste like doody, dogs would be robbing stores with guns.

— Elayne Boosler

I believe that I was a dog in a past life. That's the only thing that would explain why I like to snack on Purina Dog Chow.

— Dean Koontz

Lawyer Thoughts
@lawyerthoughts

Following

I bet my dog thinks "no more" means "at least 3 more treats are coming."

from Dave Barry

Well, Owl Be Doggone!

It seems that some Illinois legislators are upset because the state is funding a $180,000 study wherein researchers go around collecting owl vomit to see what owls eat, which could have important implications.

"Owls spit up pellets of hair, bone and teeth . . . at least once or twice a day," states the article.

This is also true of our small auxiliary dog, Zippy. His hobby is throwing up lizard parts when we're trying to eat dinner. He'll get that look of total concentration that dogs get when they have a really important task to perform, then he'll hunch his body over and walk around in a circle making a noise that sounds like "hornk." If you put him outside, he'll sit patiently by the door until you let him back inside, then he'll resume hornking. "Never throw up your lizard parts outside" is Rule No. 1 of the Dog Code of Ethics.

So, as you can imagine, our dinners have a very appetizing ambience:

MY WIFE: Would you like some more stew?

ME: Sure, I'd love . . .

ZIPPY: Hornk.

ME: On second thought . . .

ZIPPY: HORRRRNNK.

MY SON: Look! A tail and a leg!

ME: I think I'll just lie down.

— *Dave Barry Talks Back*

The Heimlich maneuver works on house pets. My pitbull was choking on his dinner. I squeezed his stomach and the neighbor's cat shot right out.

— Scott Wood

I also try very hard to never let Towhee know how much I paid for her dog food. If she hears that I bought some really cheap chow for her, she will refuse to eat it. I have to plead with her to even sniff the stuff.

— Al Batt

TRAINING DOGS

First you learn a new language, profanity; and second you learn not to discipline your dogs when you're mad, and that's most of the time when you're training dogs.

— Lou Schultz, trainer of Alaskan huskies

A well-trained dog will make no attempt to share your lunch. He will just make you feel so guilty that you cannot enjoy it.

— Helen Thomson

My dog learned how to beg by watching me through the bedroom door.

— Rodney Dangerfield

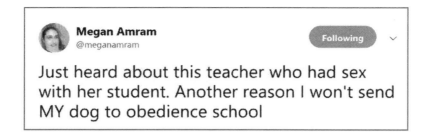

from The Onion

Tips for Training Your Dog

Bringing a dog into the family can be as difficult as it is rewarding, and pet owners must set rules and boundaries for the newest members of their household. Here are The Onion's tips for training your dog:

- Start with simple commands like "sit" before working your way up to the more complicated ones like "fill the gaping void in my life."

- Remember that consistently good behavior will take time. You're letting a fucking animal loose in your house.

- Set a good example for your dog by never chasing after squirrels, no matter how badly you want to.

- It's important to establish dominance. Show your dog who's boss by cleaning up its waste and paying for all its food.

- Consistency is key. Remember to use the same expletive every time your dog chews up your shoes.

- Dogs crave clear direction, so be sure to schedule yours for quarterly performance reviews.

- Remain patient during training sessions with your dog, as English is not its first language.

- Rather than simply saying "no" to your pet, engage it in a constructive dialogue about the moralistic implications of the undesired behavior.

from Dave Barry

Dogged Pursuits

If you were to ask me, "Dave, what are the two words that summarize everything that you truly believe in, other than that beer should always be served in a chilled glass?" I would have to respond: "Dog obedience." I own two dogs, and they have both been trained to respond immediately to my voice. For example, when we're outside, all I have to do is issue the following standard dog command: "Here Earnest! Here Zippy! C'mon! Here doggies! Here! I said come HERE! You dogs COME HERE RIGHT NOW!! ARE YOU DOGS LISTENING TO ME?? HEY!!!" And instantly both dogs, in unison, like a precision drill team, will continue trotting in random directions, sniffing the ground.

This is, of course, exactly what I want them to do. Dogs need to sniff the ground; it's how they keep abreast of current events. The ground is a giant dog newspaper, containing all kinds of late-breaking dog news items, which, if they are especially urgent, are often continued in the next yard. We live next to an aircraft carrier-sized dog named Bear who is constantly committing acts of prize-winning journalism around the neighborhood, and my dogs are major fans of his work. Each morning, while I am shouting commands at them, they race around and scrutinize the most recent installments of the ongoing Bear *oeuvre*, vibrating their bodies ecstatically to communicate their critical comments ("Bear has done it AGAIN!" "This is CLASSIC Bear!" etc.).

Of course, you cannot achieve this level of obedience overnight. You have to take the time to understand dogs as a species, to realize that they have not always been peaceful domesticated animals who fulfill their nutritional requirements primarily by sidling up to the coffee table when you're not looking and snorking taco chips directly out of the bowl. Millions of years ago dogs were fierce predators who roamed in hungry packs; if some unfortunate primitive man got caught out in the open, the dogs would surround him, knock him to the ground and, with saliva dripping from their wolf-like jaws, lick him to within an inch of his life. "Damn it, Bernice!" he would yell to primitive woman. "We got to get these dogs some professional obedience training!" This is still basically the situation today.

We had our larger dog, Earnest, professionally trained by a very knowledgeable woman who came to our house and spent several hours commanding Earnest to "heel." Wouldn't it be funny if it turned out that animals actually had high IQs and understood English perfectly, and the only reason they act stupid is that we're always giving them unintelligible commands? Like, maybe at night in the stable, the horses stand around asking each other: "What the hell does 'giddyap' mean?"

But the trainer had no trouble getting Earnest to comprehend "heel." Her technique was to give commands in a gentle but firm voice; to consistently praise Earnest for obeying properly; and every now and then, as a reminder, to send 75,000 volts of electricity down the leash. At least that's how I assume she did it, because in no time she had Earnest heeling like Vice President Quayle. Whereas when *I* take Earnest for a "walk," I am frequently yanked horizontal by dog lunges of semi-nuclear force— Earnest could tow a bulldozer across Nebraska — so that my body, clinging desperately to the leash, winds up bouncing gaily down the street behind Earnest at close to the federal speed limit, like a tin can tied to a newlywed couple's car.

But "heel" is not the only obedience skill our dogs have mastered. They also know:

ANSWER THE DOOR — When a person, real or imagined, comes to our house, both dogs charge violently at the front door barking loudly enough to shatter glass, because they know, through instinct, that there is a bad guy out there and they *must protect the house*. So when we open the door, no matter who is standing there — a neighbor, a delivery person, Charles Manson holding a four-foot machete — the dogs barge *right past him* and race outside, looking for the bad guy, who for some reason is never there, a mystery that always causes the dogs to come to skidding four-legged stops and look around with expressions of extreme puzzlement. Foiled again! He's a clever one, that bad guy!

GO TO SCHOOL — The highlight, the absolute pinnacle, of our dogs' entire existence is riding in the car when we drive our son to school, an activity that gives them the opportunity to provide vital services such as barking at policemen and smearing dog snot all over the rear window. So every morning they monitor us carefully, and the instant we do something that indicates to them that our departure is imminent, such as we wake up, they sprint to the garage door and bark at it, in case we've forgotten where it is, then they sprint back to us and bark some more, to let us know they're ready to go, and then they sprint back to the garage door, then back to us, and so on, faster and faster, until they become barely visible blurs of negative-IQ canine activity rocketing through the house at several hundred revolutions per minute. You can just imagine, then, how difficult it can be for us to make them understand the concept of "Saturday." One non-school morning my wife felt so sorry for them that she went out in her bathrobe and drove them around the neighborhood for awhile, looking for things they could bark at. So don't try to tell me dog training isn't worth it, OK? I can't hear you anyway, because there's a bad guy at the door.

— *Dave Barry Talks Back*

The truth is Pavlov's dog trained Pavlov to ring his bell just before the dog salivated.

— George Carlin

In order to really enjoy a dog, one doesn't merely try to train him to be semi-human. The point of it is to open oneself to the possibility of becoming partly a dog.

— Edward Hoagland

from The Onion

NEWS IN BRIEF

Alternative Training School For Dogs De-Emphasizes Obedience

MONTEREY, CA — Dogs who attend the Kylee Alternative Training Institute are exposed to a "creative canine learning environment where less emphasis is placed on obedience," director Morgan Kylee said Monday. "We believe in helping our students to discover their own potential, rather than forcing them to conform to the traditional idea of what a dog should be," Kylee said. "Dogs that mess on the carpet or bark incessantly are not scolded, but praised for finding their own parameters. Our motto is 'If it feels good, chew it.'" Classes at the school include Holistic Heeling, Elective Fetching, and Removing The Leg-Humping Stigma.

from The Onion

NEWS IN BRIEF

Bo Obama Addresses Graduates of Dayton Obedience School

DAYTON, OH — Calling on the 2017 class of canines to make the most of their training as they head out into the world, former first dog Bo Obama delivered a stirring commencement speech Friday to graduates of the Dayton Obedience School. "It was such an honor to have Bo Obama encouraging these fresh-faced young pups to seize their future and sit, stay, or heel as instructed," said Dayton Obedience School administrator Hannah Muley, noting that the former first dog was the school's most notable speaker since Moose from *Frasier* addressed graduates in 1998. "It was incredible to hear Bo's stories about his time in Washington and how the impulse control skills that he learned at our institution helped him overcome the adversity he faced at the White House. Here was living proof that no goal is out of reach if you're a good dog, such a good dog." The speech was not welcomed by all, however, as several of the graduating canines reportedly walked out in protest due to Bo's controversial stance on neutering.

Most owners are at length able to teach themselves to obey their dog.

— Robert Morley

MAN'S BEST FRIEND?

We are alone, absolutely alone on this chance planet: and, amid all the forms of life that surround us, not one, excepting the dog, has made an alliance with us.

— Maurice Maeterlinck

It did not take Man long — probably not more than a hundred centuries — to discover that all the animals except the dog were impossible around the house. One has but to spend a few days with an aardvark or llama, command a water buffalo to sit up and beg or try to housebreak a moose, to perceive how wisely Man set about his process of elimination and selection.

— James Thurber

Properly trained, a man can be dog's best friend.

— Corey Ford

I once had a dog who really believed he was man's best friend. He kept borrowing money from me.

— Gene Perret

I've heard that dogs are man's best friend. That explains where men are getting their hygiene tips.

— Kelly Maguire

They say a dog is a man's best friend, but I don't buy it. How many of your friends have you neutered?

— Larry Reeb

Dogs do make wonderful best friends. Dogs understand a man. A bartender has never heard a sad man tell him, "My dog doesn't understand me."

— Al Batt

It's no coincidence that man's best friend cannot talk.

— Unknown

That's why dogs are man's best friend. 'Cause guys want buddies that are dumber than they are. So do women, but they've already got men.

— Bill Engvall

Dogs: the best friend you will ever have that pees on your couch and stays your friend.

— Dana Gould

Outside of a dog, a book is probably man's best friend; inside of a dog, it's too dark to read.

— Groucho Marx

When a man's best friend is his dog, that dog has a problem.

— Edward Abbey

DOGS ARE SMART . . .
AND THAT'S WHY WE LOVE THEM

How smart are dogs?

The average dog has the mental ability of a 2-year-old. At least that's what dog IQ tests say. Dogs, moreover, spare you the terrible twos.

Which dog breed is the smartest?

Yours, of course — assuming you own a border collie.

Second and third places go to poodles and German Shepherds. All three breeds have the smarts of 2 ½-year-old kids.

Which dogs are the dumbest?

Don't get mad at the messenger. It's the hounds, the bulldog, and the beagle.

In math, dogs can compete with 3- and 4-year-olds, and in social intelligence, dogs are apparently right up there with teenagers, which may not be saying much.

Your dog, of course, is much smarter.

There is only one smartest dog in the world, and every boy has it.

— Unknown

I used to look at Smokey and think, "If you were a little smarter you could tell me what you were thinking," and he'd look at me like he was saying, "If you were a little smarter, I wouldn't have to."

— Fred Jungclaus

If you think dogs can't count, try putting three dog biscuits in your pocket and then giving Fido only two of them.

— Phil Pastoret

I'm smarter than my dogs. Well, smarter than one of my dogs.

— Ellen Degeneres, *My Point . . . And I Do Have One*

A Canadian psychologist is selling a video that teaches you how to test your dog's IQ. Here's how it works: If you spend $12.99 for the video, your dog is smarter than you.

— Jay Leno

Sometimes you panic and find yourself emitting remarks so profoundly inane that you would be embarrassed to say them to your dog. Your dog would look at you and think to itself, "I may lick myself in public, but I'd never say anything as stupid as that."

— Dave Barry

Dalmatians are not only superior to other dogs, they are like all dogs, infinitely less stupid than men.

— Eugene O'Neill

from The Onion

NEWS IN BRIEF

Police Dog Successfully Brings Down Fugitive Frisbee

COLUMBUS, OH — Columbus police commended the bravery and quick instincts of Dutch, an off-duty police dog, who pursued, apprehended, and retrieved a Frisbee that temporarily escaped the grasp of a fellow officer during a department-wide summer cookout Sunday. "The flying disk spun out of my hands shortly after I took temporary custody of same from a fellow officer," said Sgt. Vincent Visceglia, who admitted that the wanted Frisbee likely could have escaped into traffic if not for Dutch's fast actions. "Somehow Dutch knew that the Frisbee was a flight risk, so much so that he later displayed some reluctance to transfer it to authorities." Dutch, who had no comment on the incident, later grudgingly accepted a decoration for valor in secondhand baby clothing from Visceglia's daughters Eve and Cynthia.

from The Onion

NEWS IN BRIEF

Hero Dog Fills Out Hospital Paperwork

BRACKNEY, PA — Ginger, a four-year-old golden retriever, saved the life of her owner Megan Walsh, 37, Monday by quickly and efficiently filling out Walsh's copious emergency-room paperwork. "Without Ginger's knowledge of my sister's medical history, which includes multiple food allergies and penicillin intolerance, who knows what could have happened in there," said Walsh's brother Derek, who arrived late at the hospital but was relieved to learn that Ginger had "taken care of everything." "She filled out the forms, and apparently was the only one who could locate Megan's insurance card." Ginger could not be reached for comment, as she was reportedly on hold with a Blue Cross-Blue Shield phone representative for 50 minutes.

DOGS ARE DUMB . . . AND THAT'S WHY WE LOVE THEM

Even the stupidest cat seems to know more than any dog.

— Eleanor Clark

I love dogs because there's no filter mechanism between the dog's brain and its tail. There's no filter there. Like, if the dog is happy, the tail is wagging; if the tail is wagging, the dog is happy. There's no passive aggressive shit like humans, like, "Oh this douchebag thinks I'm happy to see him."

— Christian Finnegan

Dogs — putting the lie to the age-old saying, "I could never love anyone who ate a diaper."

— Dana Gould

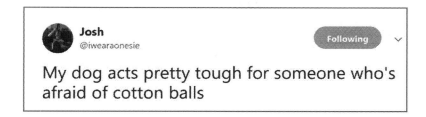

Our late lamented English setter was spoilt, goofy, terrifyingly tenacious and possessed a totally unbridled sex drive. If he got on the trail of a bitch, he would charge across three main roads, race twenty miles until he caught up with her and then mount her from the wrong end.

— Jilly Cooper

We are pretty sure that we and our pets share the same reality, until one day we come home to find that our wistful, intelligent friend who reminds us of our better self has decided a good way to spend the day is to open a box of Brillo pads, unravel a few, distribute some throughout the house, and eat or wear all the rest. And we shake our heads in an inability to comprehend what went wrong here.

— Merrill Markoe, *What The Dogs Have Taught Me*

I tried to get my dog to practice safe sex. But he keeps licking the condoms off.

— Tim Halpern

Dogs make good pets because they are very loyal. (NOTE: When I say "loyal," I mean "stupid.")

— Dave Barry

A dog is not intelligent. Never trust an animal that is surprised by its own farts.

— Frank Skinner

A watchdog is a dog kept to guard your home, usually by sleeping where a burglar would awaken the household by falling over him.

— Unknown

from Dave Barry

Earning a Collie Degree

We have a new dog, which means we're going through this phase where we spend a lot of time crouching and stroking and going "Yessss! That's a GOOD girl!" and otherwise practically awarding the Nobel Prize to her for achievements such as not pooping on the rug.

Her name is Earnest, which I realize is not a traditional girl's name, but it describes her very well. Most dogs are earnest, which is why most people like them. You can say any fool thing to a dog, and the dog will give you this look that says, "My God, you're RIGHT! I NEVER would have thought of that!" So we come to think of dogs as being understanding and loving and compassionate, and after a while we hardly even notice that they spend the bulk of their free time circling around with other dogs to see which one can sniff the other the most times in the crotch. We are not sure yet whether Earnest has a working brain. You can't tell, early on, with dogs. When we got our previous dog, Shawna, we thought she was smart as a whip, because she was a purebred German shepherd who had this extremely alert look. At first we took this to mean that she was absorbing every tiny detail of her environment with her keen senses and analyzing it with computer-like speed, but it turned out to be her way of expressing the concept: "What?"

Shawna would be sitting in our yard, looking very sharp, and a squirrel would scurry right past her, a squirrel whose presence was instantly detected by normal, neighborhood dogs hundreds of yards away, causing them to bark rigorously, and also by us humans, causing us to yell, helpfully: "Look! Shawna! A squirrel!!" And after a few seconds of delay, during which her nervous system would send the message via parcel post from her ears to her brain that something was going on, Shawna would turn in the exact opposite direction from whichever way the squirrel was, adopt a pose of great canine readiness, and go: "What?"

The only dog I ever met that was dumber than Shawna belongs to my editor. This dog, a collie named Augie, also looks smart, because you tend to think collies are smart if you grew up watching Lassie. Lassie looked brilliant, in part because the farm family she lived with was made up of idiots. Remember? One of them was always getting pinned under the tractor, and Lassie was always rushing back to the farmhouse to alert the other ones. She'd whimper and tug at their sleeves, and they'd always waste precious minutes saying things: "Do you think something's wrong? Do you think she wants us to follow her? What is it, girl?" etc., as if this had never happened before, instead of every week. What with all the time these people spent pinned under the tractor, I don't see how they managed to grow any crops whatsoever. They probably got by on federal crop supports, which Lassie filed the applications for.

So anyway I thought Augie, being a collie, would have at least some intelligence, despite the fact that when my editor and I would walk into his house, Augie would not notice us, sometimes for upwards of a half hour. When she finally did notice us, talking and drinking beer, she would bark as though the Manson gang had just burst in, so my editor would have to go over and sort of say, "Look! It's me! The person you have lived with for 10 years!" This would cause Augie's lone functioning brain cell to gradually quiet down and go back to sleep.

But I still thought she was roughly on a par with Shawna, IQ-wise, until the night — you may remember that night; it was the longest one we ever had — that I slept on my editor's couch in his living room, which is also where Augie sleeps. Only she doesn't sleep. What she does is, first, she lies down. Then she scratches herself. Then she engages in loud personal hygiene. Then she thinks, "Maybe I can go out!" and she walks across the floor, which is made of a special kind of very hard wood so that when a dog walks on it, it goes TICK TICK TICK TICK at exactly the volume you would use to get maximum benefit from the Chinese Ticking Torture. When Augie gets to the front door, which is of course closed — it is always closed at night; even the domestic insects have learned this by now — she bumps into it with her head. Then she backs up and bumps into it with her head a couple more times, in case there has been some mistake. Then she senses, somehow, that there is a person sleeping on the couch, and she has the most innovative idea she has ever thought of, which is: "Maybe he will let me out!" So she walks over to me and noses me in the face, using the same nose she uses for hygiene, and I say, "Dammit, Augie! Go to sleep!" So she lies down for one minute, which is how long it takes for her brain cell to forget everything that has ever happened to her since she was born. And then she starts again: SCRATCH SCRATCH SCRATCH SLURP SLURP SLURP (think) TICK TICK TICK TICK BUMP (think) BUMP (think) BUMP (think) TICK TICK TICK TICK NOSE "DAMMIT, AUGIE! GO TO SLEEP!" TICK TICK TICK TICK (pause) SCRATCH. . . .

I don't know yet about Earnest. One day soon I will give her the dog intelligence test, where you show her the ball, then you put the ball under a blanket, and then you see if she can find the ball. Shawna could never find the ball. I doubt Augie could find the blanket. I'm hoping Earnest does better, but I'm not counting my chickens. I am also not looking forward to receiving a lot of violent letters from you dog lovers out there, the ones with the "I (heart) my (breed of dog)" bumper stickers, asking how dare I say dogs are stupid when your dog can add, subtract, land the space shuttle, etc. So please note, dog lovers: I never said your dog is stupid. I said my dog might be stupid. I know for a fact that she can't be too intelligent, because here I've written a fairly insulting column about her species, and despite the fact that she's lying right at my feet, it hasn't occurred to her to pull the plug on my word processor.

— *Dave Barry's Greatest Hits*

from Ellen DeGeneres

Another type of animal testing that I think is really wrong is having animals take the SATs. Their scores are always so low, and it's just not fair. It makes them feel stupid, but that's only because the tests are biased toward humans. Because if you asked a person if some type of food is edible, they might not know. They'd eat it and die. An animal wouldn't do that. But if you asked a dog, "Egg is to nest as baby is to what?" it would just stare at you. Or maybe bite your leg. Or go to the bathroom on your carpet. They feel so depressed afterward, because they just don't know. You give them their score, and they just look and say, "Huh?" Then you have to say, "I'm sorry, Mr. Doggy, but you can't go to Harvard."

— *My Point . . . and I Do Have One*

I think animal testing is a terrible idea; they get all nervous and give the wrong answers.

— Unknown

from Jerry Seinfeld

Dogs Want to be People

A dog will stay stupid. That's why we love them so much. The entire time we know them, they're idiots. Think of your dog. Every time you come home, he thinks it's amazing.

He has no idea how you accomplish this every day. You walk in the door, the joy of this experience overwhelms him. He looks at you, *he's back, it's that guy, that same guy.* He can't believe it. Everything is amazing to your dog. *Another can of food? I don't believe it!*

Dogs want to be people. That's what their lives are about. They don't like being dogs. They're with people all the time, they want to graduate. My dog would sit there all day, he would watch me walk by, he would think to himself, *I could do that! He's not that good!*

That's why the greatest, most exciting moment in the life of a dog is the front seat of the car. You and him in the front seat. It's the only place where your head and his head are on the exact same level. He sits up there, he thinks, this is more like it. You and me together, this is the way it should be.

You know what cracks me up? He looks out the front. That makes me laugh, because he's a dog. What's he looking at? What are you going to make, a right or a left? I don't even know where I am.

They have a hard time. They stand up, they sit down, they can't handle the turns either way. No matter which way you turn, he's not ready.

They don't know what to do. And then comes the great moment of frustration. You stop someplace and get something to eat. This kills him. You get a hamburger, this blows his mind. Instant food when you want it? You know what this means to him? You ever see the look on his face? He looks over at you. How'd you get that? Are they giving it to everybody now? You think l could get one? I can't get one. They can't get anything.

Dogs have no money. Isn't that amazing? They're broke their entire lives. But they get through. You know why dogs have no money? No pockets.

Our dog just wanders around the house with a concerned look on his face. Dogs are just people who can't find their phone.

— Dana Gould

from Dave Barry

"Adventure Dog!"

I have this idea for a new television series. It would be a realistic action show, patterned after the true-life experiences of my dog, Earnest. The name of the show would be "Adventure Dog."

The theme song would go:

> Adventure dog,
> Adventure dooooooooggg
> Kinda big, kinda strong
> Stupid as a log.

Each episode would be about an exciting true adventure that happened to Earnest. For example, here's the script for an episode entitled: "Adventure Dog Wakes Up and Goes Outside":

It's 6:17 A.M. Adventure Dog is sleeping in the hall. Suddenly, she hears a sound. Her head snaps up. Somebody is up! Time to swing into action! Adventure Dog races down the hall and skidding on all four paws, turns into the bathroom, where, to her total shock, she finds: The Master! Whom she has not seen since LAST NIGHT!! YAYYYYYY!!

ADVENTURE DOG: Bark! Master: DOWN, dammit!

Now Adventure Dog bounds to the front door, in case the Master is going to take her outside. It is a slim chance. He has only taken her outside for the past 2,637 consecutive mornings. But just in case, Adventure Dog is ready.

ADVENTURE DOG: Bark!

Can it be? Yes! This is unbelievable! The Master is coming to the door! Looks like Adventure Dog is going outside! YAAAYYY!

MASTER: DOWN, dammit!

Now the Master has opened the door approximately one inch. Adventure Dog realizes that, at this rate, it may take the Master a full three-tenths of a second to open the door all the way. This is bad. He needs help. Adventure Dog puts her nose in the crack and applies 600,000 pounds of force to the door.

MASTER: HEY!

DOOR: WHAM!

And now Adventure Dog is through the door, looking left, looking right, her finely honed senses absorbing every detail of the environment, every nuance and subtlety, looking for . . . Holy Smoke! There it is! The YARD! Right in the exact same place where it was yesterday! This is turning out to be an UNBELIEVABLE adventure!

ADVENTURE DOG: Bark!

Adventure Dog is vaguely troubled. Some primitive version of a thought is rattling around inside her tiny cranium, like a BB in a tuna-fish can. For she senses that there is some reason why the Master has let her outside. There is something he wants Adventure Dog to do. But what on Earth could it be? Before Adventure Dog can think of an answer, she detects . . . is this possible? Yes! It's a SMELL! Yikes! Full Red Alert!

ADVENTURE DOG: Sniff sniff sniff.

MASTER: Come *on*, Earnest!

ADVENTURE DOG: Sniff sniff sniff sniff sniff sniff sniff sniff.

No question about it. The evidence is clear. This is a smell, all right. And what's more, it's the smell of — this is so incredible — DOG WEEWEE!! Right here in the yard!

MASTER: EARNEST!

ADVENTURE DOG: Sniff sniff sniff sniff sniff.

Adventure Dog is getting the germ of an idea. At first it seems farfetched, but the more she thinks about it, the more she thinks, hey, why not? The idea — get ready — Adventure Dog is going to MAKE WEEWEE!! Right now! Outside! It's crazy, but it just might work!

MASTER: Good GIRL.

What was that? It was a sound! A sound coming from over there. Yes! No question about it! This is unbelievable! It's the MASTER out here in the yard! YAAAYY!

MASTER: DOWN, dammit!

THEME SONG SINGER: Adventure Dog, Adventure Doooooggg. . . .

ADVENTURE DOG: BARK!

MASTER: DOWN!

Bear in mind that this is only one episode. There are many other possibilities: "Adventure Dog Gets Fed," "Adventure Dog Goes For a Ride in the Car and Sees Another Dog and Barks Real Loud for the Next 116 Miles," etc. It would be the kind of family-oriented show your kids could watch, because there would be extremely little sex, thanks to an earlier episode, "Adventure Dog Has An Operation."

— *Dave Barry's Greatest Hits*

Rodney Lacroix
@moooooog35
Following

Burglar: [smashes window]
Burglar: [comes into house]
Burglar: [steals electronics]
Burglar: [steals furniture]
Burglar: [steals jewelry]
Burglar: [ransacks bedrooms]
Burglar: [opens package of cheese]

My dog [coming out of my bedroom]: hey, what you got there?

from The Onion

NEWS IN BRIEF

"Lost Dog" Poster Really Tooting Dog's Horn

BROOKLYN, NY—Claiming the flyer could really stand to tone it down a little, sources said a lost dog poster that began appearing in Brooklyn's Fort Greene neighborhood Tuesday was really tooting the dog's horn. "Friendly, smart, super-sweet BAILEY," read the poster that reportedly would not shut up about the "beloved and precious" animal that, observers noted, was nevertheless somehow allowed to slip out of the house. "Responds to her name and never, ever bites!" At press time, several sources reported seeing a dog similar to Bailey running in and out of traffic like an idiot.

DOG ENTHUSIASM

Excerpts from a Dog's Diary

8:00 am   Dog food! My favorite thing!

9:30 am   A car ride! My favorite thing!

9:40 am   A walk in the park! My favorite thing!

10:30 am   Got rubbed and petted! My favorite thing!

12:00 pm   Lunch! My favorite thing!

12:30 pm   Licked myself! My favorite thing!

1:00 pm   Played in the yard! My favorite thing!

3:00 pm   Wagged my tail! My favorite thing!

5:00 pm   Milk Bones! My favorite thing!

7:00 pm   Got to play ball! My favorite thing!

8:00 pm   Wow! Watched TV with the people! My favorite thing!

11:00 pm   Sleeping on the bed! My favorite thing!

— Unknown

Blind Chow
@BlindChow

Following

dog reading birthday card
[front] Who's a good boy?
holds breath
[inside] You are!
tail goes fuckin nuts

Every time I told my cocker spaniel, Taffy, my very first dog, that we were going for a walk, she would launch into a celebratory dance that ended with her racing around the room, always clockwise, and faster and faster, as if her joy could not be possibly contained. Even as a young boy I knew that hardly any creature could express joy so vividly as a dog.

— Jeffrey Moussaieff Masson

"He means well, but this house is not his size."

Jerome K. Jerome

What I've suffered from them this morning no tongue can tell. It began with Gustavus Adolphus. Gustavus Adolphus (they call him "Gusty" downstairs for short) is a very good sort of a dog, when he is in the middle of a large field, or on a fairly extensive common, but I won't have him in-doors. He means well, but this house is not his size. He stretches himself, and over go two chairs and a what-not. He wags his tail, and the room looks as if a devastating army had marched through it. He breathes, and it puts the fire out.

At dinner-time, he creeps in under the table, lies there for a while, and then gets up suddenly; the first intimation we have of his movements being given by the table, which appears animated by a desire to turn somersaults. We all clutch at it frantically, and endeavor to maintain it in a horizontal position; whereupon his struggles, he being under the impression that some wicked conspiracy is being hatched against him, become fearful, and the final picture presented is generally that of an overturned table and a smashed-up dinner, sandwiched between two sprawling layers of infuriated men and women.

He came in this morning in his usual style, which he appears to have founded on that of an American cyclone, and the first thing he did was to sweep my coffee cup off the table with his tail, sending the contents full into the middle of my waist-coat.

— "On Cats and Dogs," *The Idle Thoughts of an Idle Fellow* (1890)

The best thing about dogs is you can act like something really good just happened and they'll instantly start celebrating. They have no idea what the context is, they're just always ready to party.

— Unknown

from The Onion

NEWS IN BRIEF

Senators Wish Domenici Would Bring Dog To Work More Often

WASHINGTON, DC — Members of the U.S. Senate wish that Sen. Pete Domenici (R-NM) would bring his sheepdog Luke to work more often, Beltway sources reported Monday. "It's always so fun when we're debating a piece of legislation, and Luke comes charging in and runs all around the Senate floor saying hi to everybody," Sen. Jon Corzine (D-NJ) said. "A couple weeks ago, I was right in the middle of a speech when he bowled me over and started licking my face." Virtually every senator has encouraged Domenici to bring in Luke, with the notable exception of Sen. Mary Landrieu (D-LA), who is "so allergic to that thing, it's not even funny."

You know the only thing happier than a three-legged dog? A four-legged dog.

— Louis C.K.

from The Onion

NEWS IN BRIEF

Dog Experiences Best Day Of His Life For 400th Consecutive Day

SANTEE, CA — Family dog Loki experienced the best day of his life for the 400th straight day Monday, the black Labrador retriever reported. "I got to go outside! I got to sniff the bush!" Loki said, wagging excitedly. "I saw a squirrel and I barked at it and it ran up the tree! Then I came back inside, and the smoky-smelling tall man let me have a little piece of bacon and then I drank from the toilet!" Loki will experience the best day of his life once again tomorrow, when he digs a hole, chews on a slipper, and almost catches his tail.

Money will buy you a pretty good dog, but it won't buy the wag of his tail.

— Josh Billings

from Merrill Markoe

I got my first dog when I was in kindergarten and instantly found his presence to be comforting and entertaining. After a long day of dealing with teachers and parents who seemed impossible to please, what a relief it was to join, in progress, a species who honestly felt at any given moment, that "this is the best moment of my life. . . Until right now, which is slightly better. . . Wait, I meant *this*. . . No, *this*. . . No, I spoke too soon. This moment right *now* is the best one ever."

— *Cool, Calm & Contentious*

DOG SHOWS

from Dave Barry

Gone to the Dogs

Recently it was my great honor to serve as a judge in the Key West Kritter Patrol Dog Show, which is considered one of the most prestigious dog shows held in the entire Key West area on that particular weekend.

This is not one of those dog shows in which serious, highly competitive dog snobs enter professional dogs that can trace their lineage back 153 generations and basically spend their entire lives sitting around being groomed and fed, like Zsa Zsa Gabor. The Key West show — it benefits the Kritter Patrol, a local group that finds people to adopt stray dogs and cats — reflects the relaxed attitude of Key West, where the term "business attire" means "wearing some kind of clothing." This is a show for regular civilian dogs, most of whom, if you had to identify them, technically, by breed, would fall under the category of: "probably some kind of dog."

These are not pampered show animals, but hard-working, highly productive dogs that spend their days industriously carrying out the vital ongoing dog mission of sniffing every object in the world, and then, depending on how it smells, either (a) barking at it; (b) eating it; (c) attempting to mate with it; (d) making weewee on it; or, in the case of small, excitable dogs, (e) all of the above.

When I arrived at the show, the last-minute preparations were proceeding with the smooth efficiency of a soccer riot. There were dozens of dogs on hand, ranging in size from what appeared to be cotton swabs with eyeballs, all the way up to Hound of the Baskervilles. Naturally every single one of these dogs, in accordance with the strict rules of dog etiquette, was dragging its owner around by the leash, trying to get a whiff of every other dog's personal region. This process was complicated by the fact that many of the dogs were wearing costumes, so they could compete in the Dog and Owner Look-Alike category. (There are a number of categories in this show, and most of the dogs compete in most of them.) Many owners were also wearing costumes, including one man with an extremely old, totally motionless, sleeping Chihuahua; the man had very elaborately dressed both the dog and himself as (why not?) butterflies. The man wore a sequined pantsuit, antennae, and a huge pair of wings.

"Look at that!" I said to the other judges, pointing to the butterfly man.

"Oh, that's Frank," several judges answered, as if this explained everything.

Perhaps you are concerned that I, a humor columnist with no formal training or expertise in the field of dogs, was on the judging panel. You will be relieved to know that there were also two professional cartoonists, Mike ("Mother Goose and Grimm") Peters and Jeff ("Shoe") MacNelly, both of whom have drawn many expert cartoons involving dogs. Another judge, named Edith, actually did seem to know a few things about dogs, but I believe she was not totally 100 percent objective, inasmuch as her own dog, Peggy, was entered in most of the events. Edith consistently gave Peggy very high ratings despite the fact that Peggy is — and I say this with great affection and respect — the ugliest dog in world history. I think she might actually be some kind of highly experimental sheep. Nevertheless, thanks in part to Edith's high marks, Peggy did very well in several categories, and actually won the Trick Dog category, even though her trick consisted of — I swear this was the whole trick — trying to kick off her underpants.

Actually, that was a pretty good trick, considering the competition. The majority of the dogs entered in the Trick Dog event did not actually perform a trick per se. Generally, the owner would bring the dog up onto the stage and wave a dog biscuit at it, or play a harmonica, or gesture, or babble ("C'mon, Ralph! C'mon boy! Sing! C'mon! Woooee! C'mon! Woooooeeeee! C'mon!") in an increasingly frantic but generally futile effort to get the dog to do whatever trick it was supposed to do, while the dog either looked on with mild interest, or attempted to get off the stage and mate with the next contestant. My personal favorite in the Trick Dog category went to a very small, very excited poodle named Bunny whose trick, as far as I could tell, consisted entirely of jumping up and down and making weewee on a towel.

As you can imagine, it was not easy serving as a judge with so many strong contestants, both on the stage and hiding under the judges' table. Nevertheless, when it was all over, approximately 43 hours after it started, we had to pick one dog as Best in Show. It was a big decision, and although there was a strong and objective push for Peggy, we decided, after agonizing for close to three-tenths of a second, to give the top prize to Sam, the old, totally motionless, sleeping Chihuahua dressed as a butterfly to match his owner, Frank. Frank got quite emotional when he accepted the trophy, and we judges were touched, although we did ask Frank to make Sam move his paw so we could see that he was, in fact, sleeping, and not actually deceased. Because you have to have standards.

— *Dave Barry Is Not Taking This Sitting Down*

DOGS & CARS

Dogs who chase cars evidently see them as large, unruly ungulates badly in need of discipline and shepherding.

— Elizabeth Marshall Thomas

I was cleaning out my car when my dog jumped in thinking we were leaving. I didn't want her to get sad — so we drove around for 20 minutes.

— Unknown

Number one way life would be different if dogs ran the world: All motorists must drive with head out window.

— David Letterman

I like driving around with my two dogs, especially on the freeways. I make them wear little hats so I can use the carpool lanes.

— Monica Piper

Better not take a dog on the space shuttle, because if he sticks his head out when you're coming home his face might burn up.

— Jack Handey, *Deep Thoughts*

WHY iT'S GREAT To BE A DOG

It's a dog's life.

That expression means a difficult, miserable, boring life. This may have been true a few hundred years ago. But today?

Not so much.

It's great to be a dog because . . .

- If it itches, you can reach it.

- And no matter where it itches, no one is offended if you scratch it in public.

- If you grow hair in unusual places, no one notices.

- No one expects you to take a bath every day.

- A wet nose is considered a sign of good health.

- Your friends think no less of you for passing gas.

- Who needs a big home entertainment system? A bone or an old shoe can entertain you for hours.

- You can spend hours just smelling stuff.

- No one ever expects you to pay for lunch or dinner. You never have to worry about table manners.

- If you gain weight, it's someone else's fault.

- It doesn't bother you if the television show is a rerun.

- It doesn't take much to make you happy. You're always excited to see the same old people. All they have to do is leave the room for five minutes and come back.

- You never get in trouble for putting your head in a stranger's lap.

- No matter where you live, you own the place.

- Every garbage can is a cold buffet.

- You can sleep late every day — you can spend all day sleeping if you want.

- No one gets angry if you fall asleep while they're talking.

— Unknown

iNSIDE THE D•G'S MIND

Do dogs think?

YES, we hear you dog owners saying. You just *know* they think.

But what?

It may be obvious to you, but it's a mystery to science.

Your average dog has a brain the size of a lemon — or a lime, if you prefer. Smaller than your brain — but it functions in similar ways, maybe because we've been evolving together for tens of thousands of years.

Humans and dogs can communicate with each other, that's for sure. But what goes on in dogs' minds? How do they see the world? What would it *feel like* to be a dog?

From the dog's point of view, his master is an elongated and abnormally cunning dog.

— Mabel Louise Robinson

I wonder what goes through his mind when he sees us peeing in his water bowl.

— Penny Ward Moser

I wonder if my dog always follows me into the bathroom because I always follow him outside and that's just how he thinks it works?

— Unknown

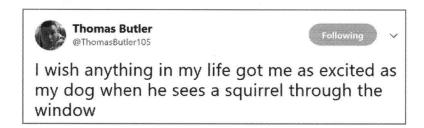

Ever consider what they must think of us? I mean, here we come back from a grocery store with the most amazing haul — chicken, pork, half a cow. They must think we're the greatest hunters on earth!

— Anne Tyler

A dog's nose is something for us to wonder at. It is perfectly remarkable and reminds us that there is a world out there that we can never know. At least not as human beings.

— Roger Caras, *A Celebration of Dogs*

from The Onion

NEWS IN BRIEF

Pet Researchers Confirm 100% Of Owners Who Leave For Work Never Coming Back

WASHINGTON — Announcing their findings amongst a series of whimpers and yelps, pet researchers confirmed Friday that 100 percent of owners who leave for work are never coming back. "Our data show conclusively that every human who says they're going to work is, in fact, gone forever the very moment they shut the door behind them," said a West Highland terrier named Nugget, adding that the findings applied equally to trips to the grocery store or the movies, both of which represented a decision to leave and never return again. "In fact, any instance in which an owner scratches a dog or cat on its head and says, 'Be back soon, buddy!' before exiting the house is a certain indication that the animal has been left to fend for itself and will eventually die unloved beside its empty food dish." At press time, an elated Nugget danced on his hind legs, reporting that 100 percent of owners who pull into the driveway at the end of the day came back for their pets after all.

from Merrill Markoe

Q. Do dogs live by a code of ethics? Are they spiritual beings?

A. Yes, they most certainly are.

Take, for example, what I like to refer to as "the cookie time incident." Every morning at my house we all wake up at six. By which I mean that they wake up at 5:45 and begin swatting me in the face and sitting on my head until I agree to get up also.

The reason that we all have to get up so early is that 6:05 is COOKIE TIME. The way this works is that at 6:00 I open the back door, and all four dogs run out into the yard to pretend to do their ablutions. Sometimes this lasts thirty seconds or less. By 6:05 cookie distribution begins.

On the day of "the incident," four dogs went out back for the pre-cookie time. But only three dogs reported, drooling and spinning, at 6:05 for cookie time.

Since it is virtually unheard of for there to be less than perfect attendance at cookie time, I knew that something was amiss. A quick check of the backyard revealed that my dog Tex, in his haste to get a good place in line at cookie time, had miscalculated his route and fallen into the pool.

My dog Tex is not my smartest dog. He has a really tentative grasp of the obvious. If he were a person, he would be Scott Baio.

By the time I got to him, he was panicky and fighting for his life as he did the "doggy magnet" — scrambling ineffectively against the slick wall of pool tiles, although he can swim.

I quickly pulled him to safety. He was fine. He shook himself off and raced into the house. Seconds later, cookie time resumed with its customary 100 percent attendance.

But, upon reflection, what impressed me was this: Moments before, the other three dogs had watched in utter silence as a member of the team fell into the pool and began to drown. They had seen his terror, they had sensed his panic and his anguish. And then, fully comprehending the gravity of the situation, they had looked at one another and thought, "Hey! It's COOKIE TIME!"

No one had thought to try to bring the matter to my attention. Not because of any lack of sensitivity, or because they are stupid and self-involved, but because, like all truly evolved creatures, they believe in accentuating the positive in a potentially tough situation. It was cookie time! Life goes on.

— *Merrill Markoe's Guide to Love*

from The Onion

NEWS IN BRIEF

Dog Trying Its Absolute Hardest

INDIANAPOLIS, IN — Woofers, the Eli family's high-spirited, 3-year-old Scottish terrier, is trying his absolute hardest at everything he does, family sources reported Monday. "Look at him," wife Jen Eli said as Woofers presented her with a tennis ball for the 22nd time that hour. "His tongue's out, his tail's wagging, he's bouncing all over the place trying to please us. There's only so much that a dog can accomplish, but Woofers is trying his best." Eli's utterance of the word "Woofers" spurred a frenzy of irrelevant leaping.

Did you ever notice when you blow in a dog's face he gets mad at you? But when you take him in a car he sticks his head out the window!

— Steve Bluestone

My dog is usually pleased with what I do, because she's not infected with the concept of what I should be doing.

— Lonzo Idolswine

from The New Yorker

Things I Want to Ask My Dog

Marsh McCall

That time I came home and the garbage was all over the kitchen floor, and you acted like you couldn't remember how it happened because you "live in the moment," did you actually remember? Be honest.

You know all those times my friends laughed at something that you were doing, like sitting upright on the sofa, or barking at the TV, and they'd say, "Look, he thinks he's a person." You don't really think you're a person, do you? Because that would be insane.

That Halloween I dressed you up like a sailor, was it humiliating? I remember my brother saying that you were clearly embarrassed. But he says a lot of things. Were you embarrassed?

Am I less authoritative when I'm naked?

Do you know you're lucky? It's important to me that you know. I'm going to show you some pictures of street dogs in Mexico.

Do you remember that fedora my brother wore for a while? Now *that* was embarrassing. I'd like to see him take care of a dog. He can't even remember if you're a boy or a girl. Just because he had a poem published in some pretentious journal doesn't mean he's got "insight." Does it?

Remember the first evening Deborah came over, and I made spaghetti, and you wandered over to the table to say hello, and she said, "I'm actually not a big fan of animals near our food," and you gave me this look, like, "Seriously? This is the one you told your mother about?" At the time I didn't think much of it, but now I'm wondering: Were you trying to warn me?

Do you think I'd look good in a fedora?

That afternoon I went to Whole Foods to return the rotten mango and, while I was gone, burglars smashed the French doors and stole my laptop, did you even try to scare them off? I like to think you did. I like to think you bared your teeth and went at them, but the truth is I came home to find you napping with your rope toy in your mouth. Whatever happened, you have to live with yourself.

Do I drink too much?

You know the time you were with me at that gas station, and I was a little preoccupied, and, after buying a bottled water, I climbed into the driver's seat of someone else's Prius, and sat you on the passenger seat, and then the owner stuck his head in the window and said, "Yo, shithead," and I screamed, "Don't hurt me"? Have you found yourself thinking less of me since then?

Back to Deborah: that morning after she moved in, and we were reading the Sunday paper in bed, and you walked over, and she said, "I'm actually not a big fan of animals in the bedroom," and you gave me another one of those looks — that was another warning, right? Bigger question: Do you actually have the ability to discern whether someone is right for me romantically? Is that a thing that animals can do, like sensing an earthquake, or hearing super-high-pitched noises? Is that why you repeatedly peed on Deborah's car tire? Or am I just shoehorning meaning into our exchanges, because it's comforting to believe that somewhere in the universe there are definitive answers to things, that there's a perfect, knowable truth, even if it's only a fleeting instinct in the mind of a dog? Do you remember the question?

When I sit down to play the piano and you leave the room before I even begin, what's that all about?

If I could make you understand that a dog's lifespan is roughly one-seventh of a human's, would you nap less?

Those times you hang out on the sofa next to me, is it because you love me, or are you worried I'll suddenly notice you're not contributing in any practical way? Do you lack purpose? Would you be happier herding sheep on a farm, or sniffing rolling suitcases at the airport? Did you know that my brother just published a novel? He sent me a copy, signed, "Best wishes." What an asshole, am I right?

The night Deborah decided to break up with me — it all began with her insisting I should move your sleeping basket to the garage, remember? She said, "I'm actually not a big fan of the dog smell in this house." And I said, "I'm actually not a big fan of the expression 'not a big fan,'" and she gasped, and I glanced at you, and I could swear you were laughing. You were, right?

Should I call Deborah?

Do you understand English?

Where are you going?

Dogs, the foremost snobs in creation, are quick to notice the difference between a well-clad and a disreputable stranger.

— Albert Payson Terhune

from The Onion

NEWS IN BRIEF

Dog Doesn't Consider Itself Part Of Family

THOMASVILLE, GA — While admitting that he relies on members of the family for food and shelter and is often included in household activities and family photographs, local 6-year-old golden retriever Pepper told reporters Friday that he in no way considers himself part of the O'Donnell family. "Hey, they're not bad people, and I appreciate that they let me ride in the car sometimes, but do I think of them as my own family members? God, no," the canine said while scratching behind his right ear with his hind leg, adding that he had no say in the matter when he was adopted and spends as much time as possible in the backyard to distance himself from the O'Donnells. "Have you seen these guys? They're kind of loud and obnoxious, they sit on that couch all the time looking at their phones, and they're not at all into throwing around the tennis ball. Just look at [father] Rob [O'Donnell] — guy's a complete mess and can't even walk to the park without getting winded. No way I'm one of them." At press time, Pepper's stance was reaffirmed when Denise O'Donnell made him sit and beg for several moments before letting him have a piece of cheese.

from George Carlin

Dogs' endearing lack of inhibition

Like I say, he'll do anything at any time. He might even embarrass you when you have company.

You might have some folks over to the house; folks you don't know that well; people you're trying to impress. . . .

And all these people are sitting around the living room, and you've put out some chips and a little dip, carrot sticks, maybe a little light buffet, and everybody is eating nicely and chatting politely, and the dog is lying there on the floor, in full view.

And suddenly, you glance over, and realize that the dog . . . is licking . . . his balls! Vigorously! Big, long, loving licks, in full view of everyone. And no one is saying a word.

Remember now, a spectacular thing is taking place: a naked, living creature is administering a modified form of autofellatio in the presence of strangers. Not only is it a spectacular act, it's difficult to do. If I could do that I'd never leave the house.

— *Napalm & Silly Putty*

Dogs act exactly the way we would act if we had no shame.

— Cynthia Heimel

from The Onion

Nation's Dogs Dangerously Underpetted, Say Dogs

NEW YORK — At a press conference Monday, representatives of the Association of American Dogs announced that the nation's canines are dangerously underpetted. "Every night, thousands of U.S. dogs go to bed without so much as a scratch behind the ears," AAD president Banjo said. "If this sort of neglect from our masters continues, it could lead to widespread jumping on the furniture." Upon his owner's arrival in the press-conference room, Banjo abruptly ended his speech, frantically barking, leaping, and rolling over on his back in an effort to communicate his need for a vigorous belly rub.

But with dogs, we do have "bad dog." Bad dog exists.

"Bad dog! Bad dog! Stole a biscuit, bad dog!"

The dog is saying, "Who are you to judge me? You human beings who've had genocide, war against people of different creeds, colors, religions, and I stole a biscuit?! Is that a crime? People of the world!"

"Well, if you put it that way, I think you've got a point. Have another biscuit, sorry."

— Eddie Izzard

from George Carlin

Fido Doesn't Care

Dogs have no priorities or schedules. You rarely see a dog with a wristwatch. Most things they do they will do anywhere, at any time. Except for the things you teach them not to do:

"Laszlo! Don't ever do that again. If you do I'll beat the shit out of you!"

They do catch on to suggestions like that.

But basically, a dog doesn't care what he does. He'll simply do whatever's next. He doesn't really know what's next, but he'll think of something.

He might even do two things in a row that don't go together. Did y'ever see a dog trotting through a room, apparently headed somewhere, and suddenly he stops and chews his back for about eight minutes? As if the whole thing were scheduled for that exact moment? And then finally, when he's finished chewing, he forgets where he was going in the first place and just sort of looks around, confused.

"Let's see, where was I goin'? Shit, I forget. Seemed important at the time. Well, I guess I'll just lie down here under this chair. Hey, it's nice under here. I must do this more often."

He doesn't know, and he doesn't care.

— *Napalm & Silly Putty*

I pick dogs that remind me of myself — scrappy, mutt-faced, with a hint of mange. People look for a reflection of their own personalities or the person they dream of being in the eyes of an animal companion. That is the reason I sometimes look into the face of my dog Stan and see wistful sadness and existential angst, when all he is actually doing is slowly scanning the ceiling for flies.

— Merrill Markoe, *What The Dogs Have Taught Me*

The doors of dogs' perception

A door is what dogs are perpetually on the wrong side of.

— Ogden Nash

Happiness to a dog is what lies on the other side of a door.

— Charleton Ogburn, Jr.

Did you ever walk into a room and forget why you walked in? I think that's how dogs spend their lives.

— Sue Murphy

from The Onion

NEWS IN BRIEF

Dog Meets Owner At Door In Desperate Attempt To Get Ahead Of Diarrhea-Rug Scandal

KENNEWICK, WA—Deftly maneuvering to control the emotional tone and establish the primacy of her own narrative before the story got out of control, 3-year-old Jack Russell terrier Muffin met her owner at the door upon his return from work Monday in a desperate attempt to get ahead of an unfolding diarrhea-riddled-living-room-rug scandal. The companion animal reportedly took quick action by enthusiastically leaping at her owner while wagging her tail and whining with supposed joy, attempting to mitigate the coming fallout over the discovery of the 2-by-5-foot slick of fecal liquefaction slowly drying mere feet away, and to present herself in the most positive light by nuzzling her owner's arm and licking his face. Moreover, Muffin immediately initiated a counter-narrative by scampering off to the dining room, grabbing the stuffed giraffe, and presenting it to her owner in a manner suggesting they play tug-of-war with the toy, evidently hoping that the creation of a favorable emotional atmosphere would soften the impact of the reeking cloud already wafting in from the next room. At press time, a severely chastised Muffin had instituted a total media blackout from beneath the bed, refusing to comment on her owner's disastrous slipping in the noisome, viscous mass or take any responsibility for the shirt and pants destroyed during his subsequent fall.

from The Dog

How you humans annoy me

- Dog sweaters. Hello? Have you noticed the fur?

- Yelling at me for barking. News flash, genius: I'm a dog.

- Taking me for a walk, then not letting me check stuff out. Whose walk is this, anyway?

- Any trick that involves balancing food on my nose. Just stop it.

- Any haircut that involves bows or ribbons. Now you know why we chew your stuff up when you're not home.

- Yelling at me for dragging my butt across your carpet. Why'd you buy carpet?

- Getting upset when I sniff your guests' crotches. Sorry, but I haven't quite mastered that handshake thing yet.

- Acting disgusted when I lick myself. We both know the truth — you're jealous.

- Picking up the poop piles in the yard. Do you realize how far behind schedule that puts me?

- Taking me to the vet for "the big snip" — then acting surprised when I don't want to go back.

- Blaming your farts on me. Not funny.

- Leaving the toilet seat down. How else am I going to get a cool drink of water?

- The sleight of hand, the fake fetch throw. Wow — you fooled a dog! What a proud moment for the top of the food chain.

— Unknown

DOG RULES AND LAWS

FROM DOGS TO DOGS

Basic Rules for Dogs Who Have a Yard to Protect

Gary Bogue

1. **Newspapers** — If you have to go pee while playing in the front yard, always use the newspaper that's placed on the driveway every morning just for that purpose.

2. **Visitors** — Quickly determine which guest is afraid of dogs. Charge across the room, barking loudly, & leap playfully on this person. If your human falls down on the floor & starts crying, lick his/her face & growl gently to show your concern.

3. **Licking** — Always take a BIG drink from your water dish immediately before licking your human. Humans always prefer clean tongues.

4. **Barking** — Because we are dogs, we are expected to bark. So bark — a lot. Your owners will be very happy to hear you protecting their

house. Especially late at night while they are sleeping safely in their beds. There is no more secure feeling for humans than to keep waking up in the middle of the night & hearing their protective dog barking and barking and . . .

5. **Holes** — There are never enough holes in the ground. Strive daily to do your part to help correct this problem. Rather than digging a BIG hole in the middle of the yard & upsetting your humans, dig a lot of small holes all over the yard so they won't notice.

6. **Doors** — The area immediately in front of a door is always reserved for the family dog to sleep on. Wag your tail so it makes tolerant, thumping sounds on the floor every time you are stepped on.

7. **Sniffing** — Humans like to be sniffed. Everywhere. It is your duty as the family dog to accommodate them.

8. **Dining** — Always sit under the table at dinner, especially when there are guests, so you can clean up food when it starts to accumulate on the floor. This is also a good time to practice your sniffing.

9. **Housebreaking** — This is very important to humans, so break as much of the house as possible.

10. **Walks** — When out for a walk with your master or mistress, never go to the bathroom on your own lawn. Always pick the nosy neighbor's yard.

11. **Couches** — It is permissible to sleep on the new couch after your humans have gone to bed.

12. **Cats** — When chasing cats, never catch them. It spoils all the fun.

FROM HUMAN OWNERS TO THEIR DOGS

Rules of the House for Dogs

- Dogs are never permitted in the house. The dog stays outside in a specially built wooden compartment — named, for very good reason, the dog house.

- OK, the dog can enter the house, but only for short visits or if his own house is under renovation.

- OK, the dog can stay in the house on a permanent basis, provided his dog house can be sold in a yard sale to a rookie dog owner.

- Inside the house, the dog is not allowed to run free and is confined to a comfortable but secure metal cage.

- OK, the cage becomes part of a two-for-one deal along with the dog house in the yard sale and the dog can go wherever the hell he pleases.

- The dog is never allowed on the furniture.

- OK, the dog can get on the old furniture but not the new furniture.

- Okay, the dog can get up on the new furniture until it looks like the old furniture and then we'll sell the whole damn works and buy new furniture . . . upon which the dog will most definitely not be allowed!

- The dog never sleeps on the bed. Period.

- OK, the dog can sleep at the foot of the bed.

- OK, the dog can sleep alongside you, but he's not allowed under the covers.

- OK, the dog can sleep under the covers but not with his head on the pillow.

- OK, the dog can sleep alongside you under the covers with his head on the pillow, but if he snores or farts, he's got to leave the room.

- OK, the dog can sleep and snore and fart and have nightmares in bed, but he's not to come in and sleep on the couch in the TV room, where I'm now sleeping. That's just not fair.

- The dog never gets listed on the census questionnaire as "primary resident," even if it's true.

— Unknown

FROM A DOG TO HERSELF

A dog's New Year's resolutions

- I will not bark each time I hear a doorbell on television.

- I will not greet visitors by sticking my nose near their privates.

- I will not throw up on carpet or in the car.

- I will not roll on dead seagulls, fish, crabs, etc.

- I will not touch other animals' poop.

- I will not wake my people up by sticking my wet nose in their ears.

- I will not chew my human's toothbrush and not tell them.

- I will not insist on having the car window rolled down when it's raining.

- I will not drop soggy tennis balls in the underwear of anyone using the toilet.

- I will not suddenly stand straight up when I'm lying under the coffee table.

- I will not roll my toys behind the fridge.

- I will shake the rainwater out of my fur before I enter the house.

- I will not offer my human assistance in emptying garbage cans.

— Unknown

FROM A DOG TO HIMSELF

Important things that I, the dog, need to remember

- The garbage collector is not stealing our stuff.

- The pizza delivery person is not a murderer.

- The diaper pail is not a cookie jar.

- The sofa is not a face towel.

- The toilet is not my water bowl.

- The cat is not a squeaky toy.

- The cat's food is not my food.

- The computer mouse is not edible.

- My head does not belong in the fridge.

— Unknown

FROM AN OWNER TO HER DOGS

Letter to My Dogs

Dear Dogs,

I'm writing to make clear my expectations for you. They are simple and, I hope you'll agree, reasonable. It would be most helpful if you would kindly abide by these modest requests.

When I say to move, it means go someplace else, not switch positions with each other so there are still two dogs in the way.

The dishes with the paw print are yours and contain your food. The other dishes are mine and contain my food. Please note, placing a paw print in the middle of my plate and food does not stake a claim for it becoming your food and dish, nor do I find that aesthetically pleasing in the slightest.

The stairway was not designed by NASCAR and is not a racetrack. Beating me to the bottom is not the object. Tripping me doesn't help, because I fall faster than you can run.

I cannot buy anything bigger than a king-size bed. I am very sorry about this. Do not think I will continue to sleep on the couch to ensure your comfort. Look at videos of dogs sleeping — they can actually curl up in a ball. It is not necessary to sleep perpendicular to each other stretched out to the fullest extent possible. I also know that sticking tails straight out and having tongues hanging out the other end to maximize space used is nothing but doggy sarcasm.

For the last time, there is not a secret exit from the bathroom. If by some miracle I beat you there and manage to get the door shut, it is not necessary to claw, whine, try to turn the knob, or get your paw under the edge and try to pull the door open. I must exit through the same door I entered. In addition, I have been using bathrooms for years — canine attendance is not mandatory.

The proper order is kiss me, then go smell the other dogs' behinds. I cannot stress this enough.

Thank you for your cooperation.

— Unknown

FROM DOGS TO EVERYONE

Dog property laws

- If I like it, it's mine.

- If it's edible, it's mine.

- If it's in my mouth, it's mine.

- If I spit it out, it's still mine.

- If I had it a little while ago, it's mine.

- If I can take it from you, it's mine.

- If you're playing with something and put it down, it's mine.

- If I'm chewing something up, all the pieces are mine.

- If I get tired of it, it's yours.

- If I want it back, it's mine.

— Unknown

FROM A DOG OWNER TO VISITORS

Notice to People Who Visit My Home

- The dog lives here. You don't.

- Of course she smells like a dog.

- If you don't want dog hair on your clothes, stay off the furniture.

- Yes, she has some odd habits. So do I and so do you.

- It's her nature to try to sniff your crotch. Feel free to sniff hers.

- I like my dog a lot better than I like most people.

- To you, she's a dog. To me, she's an adopted daughter who is short, furry, walks on all fours, and doesn't speak so clearly — and I love her.

No animal should ever jump up on the dining-room furniture unless absolutely certain that he can hold his own in the conversation.

— Fran Lebowitz

DOGS & SLEDS

from The Onion

NEWS

Stumbling, Bumbling Sled Dog: "Sorry, This Is My First Iditarod"

PUNTILLA LAKE, AK — After running directly into the grandstands during the Iditarod's ceremonial start and veering 55 miles off course late Tuesday to chase a marmot, Siberian husky and rookie sled dog Melvin apologized to his musher and fellow canines Wednesday for making a complete fool of himself in the early stages of the annual 1,150-mile race.

"First Iditarod jitters, I guess," the visibly contrite Melvin told reporters Wednesday at the Rainy Pass checkpoint. "I feel like such a moron. Here I am in the last great race on earth and I'm blowing it. I mean, 100 times out of 100, when my musher yells, 'Gee,' I turn right. But yesterday I go left down an icy slope into a bunch of evergreens and nearly break everyone's neck."

"I have to pull it together," added the dog, making a point of directly addressing his musher, two-time Iditarod champion Lance Mackey. "I'm sorry, Lance. I'm acting like an idiot out there."

Melvin has gotten his squad into several embarrassing scrapes thus far, one of which occurred at Willow Lake when, in an effort to find a place to nap, he twirled around three times while still in full harness, fouling his lines and entangling his team in multiple snarls. In addition, as the team was on route to Skwentna, a child spectator threw an imaginary stick over the team, and Melvin chased it 300 miles back to the first checkpoint at Yentna Station.

Melvin's most humiliating experience, sources said, was a 20-minute period during which Mackey repeatedly ordered him to mush and the husky merely stood motionless, staring at Finger Lake.

"You look around and you realize that you are going up against your idols — Larry, Bronte, Salem, Handsome, Blue — and then it hits you: This is the fucking Iditarod," Melvin said. "It's not the Jack Pine 30 or the American Dog Derby. Out here, if you playfully root through your musher's sled basket and destroy his heavy parka and extra-warm sleeping bag, well, that's a mistake that could haunt you the rest of your career. Unfortunately, I'm learning that the hard way."

Melvin later admitted that he was overwhelmed by the pressure of participating in his first Iditarod and consequently had psyched himself out. Bouts of anxiety reportedly led to a stress dream Monday night in which he found himself standing on a calm, ice-covered pond for several tranquil minutes before the ice suddenly cracked beneath him.

"Instantly, I was treading in freezing water, and the more I struggled to get back on land, the faster I sank," Melvin said.

As he dreamt, the husky unconsciously gnawed through his team's snub line. Consequently, two point dogs and one wheel dog are still missing, and the sled can no longer go around corners.

Just five days into the race, the group is a projected seven days behind the rest of the pack.

"I'm too 'in my head' right now, you know? I have to remember my training from when I was a pup and just be natural," said the dog, adding that despite his most recent failures, he believes he was born for this. "No more stopping in the middle of a run to find a private place to go to the bathroom. Why would I even do that? I know I'm running in the Iditarod, for crying out loud. And I'm certainly not going to sprint into my teammates ever again, because that means I'm destroying our neck and tug lines, and I'm going completely the wrong way."

"I need to stay focused," Melvin continued. "Also, I think I'm going to go chase that big moose over there."

Despite the husky's shortcomings, musher Lance Mackey has stated that Melvin will remain in the lead dog position, mainly because Melvin bit the leg of fellow lead dog Sarah. Melvin was quick to point out, however, that at the time of the incident, he was suffering a panic-related delusion in which Sarah had transformed into his father, an Alaskan malamute who always told his son he would never amount to anything.

"It's a saying amongst us mushers that the dogs never make mistakes," Mackey said. "But it's not my fault that Melvin stops every 45 minutes to furiously dig in the snow. That dog's a wreck."

Mackey then sighed and added, "This is a terrible Iditarod."

Cats are smarter than dogs. You can't get eight cats to pull a sled through snow.

— Jeff Valdez

Life is like a dogsled team. If you ain't the lead dog, the scenery never changes.

— Lewis Grizzard

SEEING EYE DOGS

I bought my grandmother a Seeing Eye dog. But he's a little sadistic. He does impressions of cars screeching to a halt.

— Larry Amoros

I asked this woman why she had two Seeing Eye dogs, and she said one was for reading.

— Jonathan Katz

I've been on so many blind dates, I should get a free dog.

— Wendy Liebman

DOG HAIKU

I love my master;
Thus I perfume myself with
This long-rotten squirrel.

I lie belly-up
In the sunshine, happier than
You ever will be.

Today I sniffed
Many dog behinds — I celebrate
By kissing your face.

I sound the alarm!
Garbage man — come to kill us all —
Look! Look! Look! Look! Look!

I lift my leg and
Whiz on each bush. Hello, Spot —
Sniff this and weep.

How do I love thee?
The ways are numberless as
My hairs on the rug.

My human is home!
I am so ecstatic I have
Made a puddle.

I hate my choke chain —
Look, world, they strangle me!
Ack Ack Ack Ack Ack Ack!

Sleeping here, my chin
On your foot — no greater bliss — well,
Maybe catching rats.

Look in my eyes and
Deny it. No human could
Love you as much as I do.

The cat is not all
Bad — she fills the litter box
With Tootsie Rolls.

Dig under fence — why?
Because it's there. Because it's
there. Because it's there.

I am your best friend,
Now, always, especially
When you are eating.

My owners' mood is
Romantic — I lie near their
Feet. I fart a big one.

— Unknown

DOG LETTERS TO GOD

Dear God,

How come people love to smell flowers, but seldom smell one another? Where are their priorities?

Dear God,

When we get to Heaven, can we sit on your couch? Or is it the same old story?

Dear God,

Excuse me, but why are there cars named after the jaguar, the cougar, the mustang, the colt, the stingray, and the rabbit, but not one named for a dog? How often do you see a cougar riding around? We dogs love a nice ride! I know every breed cannot have its own model, but it would be easy to rename the Chrysler Eagle the Chrysler Beagle!

Dear God,

If a dog barks his head off in the forest and no human hears him, is he still a bad dog?

Dear God,

Is it true that in Heaven, dining room tables have onramps?

Dear God,

If we come back as humans, is that good or bad?

Dear God,

More meatballs, less spaghetti, please.

Dear God,

We dogs can understand human verbal instructions, hand signals, whistles, horns, clickers, beepers, scent IDs, electromagnetic energy fields, and Frisbee flight paths. What do humans understand?

Dear God,

When we get to the Pearly Gates, do we have to shake hands to get in?

Dear God,

Are there dogs on other planets or are we alone? I have been howling at the moon and stars for a long time, but all I ever hear back is the beagle across the street!

Dear God,

Are there mailmen in Heaven? If there are, will I have to apologize?

Dear God,

Is it true that dogs are not allowed in restaurants because we can't make up our minds what NOT to order? Or is it the carpets thing, again?

Dear God,

May I have my testicles back?

— Unknown

THE WORLD IS MY PRIVY

from The Onion

NEWS IN BRIEF

Dog Finds Absolutely Perfect Place To Shit

PORTLAND, OR — After carefully examining every inch of sidewalk within a four block radius of his home Tuesday, local dog Sigmund, 4, finally found the absolutely perfect place to squat down on his hind legs and void his bowels. The Labrador Retriever mix — who bypassed a series of nearly perfect spots to deposit his feces — scanned the ground for a full seven minutes before eventually locating the 4-by-5-inch region that exhibited an ideal synthesis of ground texture, smell, and plant-life proximity. Sigmund then carefully strained out two and one quarter lengths of excrement onto the ideal site, approximately 11 inches from the curb and 4 inches from a street sign soaked in another dog's urine. This marked Sigmund's most successful location hunt today, surpassing an earlier incident in which the dog found a pretty okay place to vomit.

The objective is not so much to walk your dog, as it is to empty him.

— Dave Barry

The trees in Siberia are miles apart — that is why the dogs are so fast.

— Bob Hope

My dogs love me. Of course, by "love" I mean "poop" and by "me" I mean "everywhere."

— Dana Gould

from Jerry Seinfeld

On my block, a lot of people walk their dogs and I always see them walking along with their little poop bags. This, to me, is the lowest activity in human life. Following a dog with a little scooper. Waiting for him to go so you can walk down the street with it in your bag. If aliens are watching this through telescopes, they're going to think the dogs are the leaders of the planet. If you see two life forms, one of them's making a poop, the other one's carrying it for him, who would you assume is in charge?

I say, if this is where we're at after 50,000 years of civilization, let's just give up. I'm serious, let's pack it in. It's not worth it. Let's just say the human race as an idea didn't quite work. It seemed good at first, we worked on it for a long time, but it just didn't pan out. We went to the moon but still somehow wound up carrying little bags of dog doody around with us. We just got mixed up somewhere. Let's just give it over to the insects or whoever else is next in line.

— *SeinLanguage*

Some dog I got too. We call him Egypt. Because in every room he leaves a pyramid.

— Rodney Dangerfield

from Dave Barry

My major experience with moving a pet was the time we moved our dog, Earnest, from Pennsylvania to Florida via airplane. We took her to these professional pet transporters, who told us that for $357.12, which is approximately $357.12 more than we originally paid for Earnest, they would put her on the airplane in a special cage, which we would get to keep. The reason for this generosity became clear when I picked Earnest up at the Miami airport. It had been a long flight, and since Earnest had had nothing to read, she had passed the time by pooping, so you can imagine what the inside of her cage looked and smelled like, on top of which, as soon as she saw me, she went into the classic Dance of Lunatic Unrestrained Dog Joy Upon Sighting the Master, yelping and whirling like the agitator on an unbalanced washing machine, creating a veritable poop tornado inside the cage, just dying to get out and say hi.

— *Homes and Other Black Holes*

Josh Gondelman ✔
@joshgondelman

Following ⌄

I have moved into apartments after less careful consideration than my dog gives where she's going to poop on the sidewalk.

The other day I saw two dogs walk over to a parking meter. One of them says to the other, "How do you like that? Pay toilets!"

— Dave Star

THE BREEDING EDGE

If you can't decide between a Shepherd, a Setter, or a Poodle, get them all — adopt a mutt!

— ASPCA

He wa'n't no common dog, he wa'n't no mongrel; he was a composite. A composite dog is a dog that is made up of all the valuable qualities that's in the dog breed — kind of a syndicate; and a mongrel is made up of all riffraff that's left over.

— Mark Twain

Speak softly and own a big, mean Doberman.

— Dave Millman

Chi-WOW-a!

I hope if dogs ever take over the world, and they chose a king, they don't just go by size, because I bet there are some Chihuahuas with some good ideas.

— Jack Handey, *Deep Thoughts*

I've got a Chihuahua. They're good. If you lose one, just empty out your purse.

— Jean Carroll

from Dave Barry

When I say "dogs," I'm talking about dogs, which are large, bounding, salivating animals, usually with bad breath. I am not talking about those little squeaky things you can hold on your lap and carry around. Zoologically speaking, these are not dogs at all; they are members of the pillow family.

— *Dave Barry's Bad Habits*

We will retrieve. We will retrieve.

Try throwing a ball just once for a dog. It would be like eating only one peanut or potato chip. Try to ignore the importuning of a Golden Retriever who has brought you his tennis ball, the greatest treasure he possesses.

— Roger Caras, *A Celebration of Dogs*

Got a new dog . . . a paranoid retriever. He brings back everything because he's not sure what I threw.

— Steven Wright

My Labrador Retriever had a nervous breakdown. I kept throwing him a boomerang.

— Nick Arnette

Pit-Bullied

If a Pitbull romances your leg, fake an orgasm.

— Hut Landon

I have a great dog. She's half Lab, half Pitbull. A good combination. Sure, she might bite off my leg, but she'll bring it back to me.

— Jimi Celeste

I have a dog that's half Pitbull, half Poodle. Not much of a guard dog, but a vicious gossip.

— Craig Shoemaker

Poodlerized

He's SMALL.

He's BLACK.

He's MAD AS HELL.

He's POODLE with a MOHAWK.

You'll never call him Fifi again.

— Lynda Barry

I wonder if other dogs think Poodles are members of a weird religious cult.

— Rita Rudner

Pomeranians speak only to Poodles, and Poodles speak only to God.

— Charles Kuralt

Dachsundized

Dachshund: A half-a-dog high and a dog-and-a-half long.

— H.L. Mencken

Dachshunds are ideal dogs for small children, as they are already stretched and pulled to such a length that the child cannot do much harm one way or the other.

— Robert Benchley

I have a dog so mean, he ate the neighbor's weenie dog. Now he's a bratweiler.

— Nick Arnette

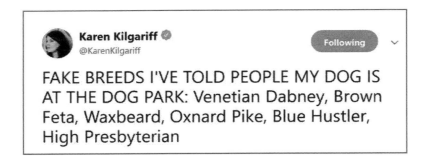

from Clickhole

How many of these dog breeds do you know?

Can you tell a Swiss thin face from an anger mule? Find out just how much of a dog lover you are — check off all of the dog breeds you know:

- The Irish no-bones

- Bearded moron

- Mushroom-lipped terrier

- Siberian Gordon

- The Sussex abomination

- Dog from the beans commercial

- American shouting dog

- Curly-necked retriever

- Regular

- Alaskan midwife

- Jack Russell terrier (Taliban-bred)

- Sleek brown

- Coughing terriers

- Ron's dog

- Newark Airport terrier

- Long-haired Fantano

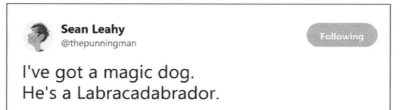

Sean Leahy
@thepunningman

Following

I've got a magic dog.
He's a Labracadabrador.

The new breeds

The following breeds are now recognized by the American Kennel Club (AKC):

Collie + Lhasa Paso =
. . . Collapso, a dog that folds up for easy transport

Spitz + Chow Chow =
. . . Spitz-Chow, a dog that throws up a lot

Pointer + Setter =
. . . Poinsetter, a traditional Christmas pet

Great Pyrenees + Dachshund =
. . . Pyradachs, a puzzling breed

Pekingese + Lhasa Apso =
. . . Peekasso, an abstract dog

Irish Water Spaniel + English Springer Spaniel =
. . . Irish Springer, a dog fresh and clean as a whistle

Labrador Retriever + Curly Coated Retriever =
. . . Lab Coat Retriever, the choice of research scientists

Newfoundland + Basset Hound =
. . . Newfound Asset Hound, a dog for financial advisors

Terrier + Bulldog =
. . . Terribull, a dog prone to awful mistakes

Bloodhound + Labrador =
. . . Blabador, a dog that barks incessantly

Malamute + Pointer =
. . . Moot Point, owned by . . . oh, well, it doesn't matter anyway

Collie + Malamute =
. . . Commute, a dog that travels to work

Deerhound + Terrier =
. . . Derriere, a dog that's true to the end

Maltese + any other breed =
. . . Maltese Cross

Kerry Blue Terrier + Skye Terrier =
. . . Blue Skye, a dog for visionaries

Cocker Spaniel + Maltese =
. . . Cocktese

Smooth Fox Terrier + Chow Chow =
. . . Smooch, a dog that loves kissing

Keeshond + Setter =
. . . Keester, a dog that won't get off its duff

Bloodhound + Borzoi =
. . . Bloody Bore, a dog that's not much fun

Bull terrier + Shitzu =
. . . A boasting, talkative breed

How many dogs does it take to change a lightbulb?

Golden Retriever — The sun is shining, the day is young, we've got our whole lives ahead of us, and you're inside worrying about a burned out bulb?

Border Collie — Just one. And then I'll replace any wiring that's not up to code.

Malamute — Let the Border Collie do it. You can feed me while he's busy.

Poodle — I'll just blow in the Border Collie's ear and he'll do it. By the time he finishes rewiring the house, my nails will be dry.

Dachshund — You know I can't reach that stupid lamp!

Rottweiler — Make me.

Lab — Oh, me! Me!! Pleeeeease let me change the light bulb! Can I? Can I? Huh? Huh? Huh? Can I?

German Shepherd — I'll change it as soon as I've led these people from the dark, check to make sure I haven't missed any, and make just one more perimeter patrol to see that no one has tried to take advantage of the situation.

Jack Russell Terrier — I'll just pop it in while I'm bouncing off the walls and furniture.

Cocker Spaniel — Why change it? I can still pee on the carpet in the dark.

Doberman Pinscher — While it's dark, I'm going to sleep on the couch.

Maltese — Who cares? I can still play with my squeaky toys in the dark.

Mastiff — Mastiffs are NOT afraid of the dark.

Chihuahua — Yo quiero Taco Bulb.

Irish Wolfhound — Can somebody else do it? I've got this hangover.

Pointer — I see it, there it is, there it is, right there.

Greyhound — It isn't moving. Who cares?

Australian Shepherd — First, I'll put all the light bulbs in a little circle. . . .

Old English Sheepdog — Light bulb? I'm sorry, but I don't see a light bulb.

Hound dog — ZZZZZZZZZzzzzzzzzz.z.z.z..z..z..z...z

— Unknown

The Airedale . . . an unrivaled mixture of brains and clownish wit, the very ingredients one looks for in a spouse.

— Chip Brown

It sometimes takes days, even weeks, before a dog's nerves tire. In the case of terriers it can run into months.

— E.B. White

Newfoundland dogs are good to save children from drowning, but you must have a pond of water handy and a child, or else there will be no profit in boarding a Newfoundland.

— Josh Billings

from The Onion

NEWS IN BRIEF

Nation Demands More Slow-Motion Footage Of Running Basset Hounds

WASHINGTON — Insisting that the dogs be filmed not only more frequently but also in the most adorable manner possible, the American populace on Friday demanded more slow-motion footage of running basset hounds. "We're calling for a dramatic increase in the number of slo-mo videos featuring droopy basset hounds racing toward the camera," said Montana resident Peter Tomsett, echoing the sentiment of all 323 million Americans who declared it was urgent that they see curtains of skin flapping, ears waving back and forth, and drool slopping everywhere as the dogs bound through a field at a fraction of their real-life speed. "I've definitely seen a slowed-down video of a couple of basset hounds running with their tongues lolling out the sides of their mouths while the *Chariots of Fire* theme played in the background, but there needs to be so many more videos like this, and they need to be made soon. It doesn't matter if they're puppies or old dogs or a mix of the two. What matters is that production of the slow-motion basset hound footage commences immediately and continues indefinitely." At press time, the entire nation was just as insistent on needing additional slow-motion shots of wet bassets hounds shaking water off their bodies.

Oh, that dog! Ever hear of a German Shepherd that bites its nails? Barks with a lisp? You say, "Attack!" And he has one. All he does is piddle. He's nothing but a fur-covered kidney that barks.

— Phillis Diller

A Pekingese is not a pet dog; he is an undersized lion.

— A.A. Milne

My father was a Saint Bernard, my mother was a Collie, but I am a Presbyterian.

— Mark Twain

In Praise of the Pug

Robert Wilde

What kind of dog is a PUG?
With its face like a wrinkled-up rug,
    Its muscular frame,
    Its punching, punk name —
You'd think that this thing was a thug

The pug is a pugilist, surely —
Gnarly and snarly and surly
    Pugs are pugnacious —
    They *must* be — good gracious!
Just look at their tails — short and curly!

That point of view would be wrong
Yes, pugs are sturdy and strong —
    But they're cheerful and charming
    Devoted, disarming —
A bundle of fun all day long

Frolicsome, friendly, outgoing
Puppyhood never outgrowing —
    The eyes? They're bright beauties
    The pugmarks? They're cuties
The face? So expressive, so knowing

Pugs adore kids — it's well known
And people even when grown
    Other dogs? *Yes!*
    Cats? You can guess —
Pugs are the puppies to own

You'll dress them — if dress them you must —
In puggarees (not sweaters, we trust)
    And please never puggle them —
    Just nuzzle and snuggle them —
Hopefully hearts will not bust

Live to love and be loved — that's our pug —
And if people out somewhere should shrug?
    Pug owners care not —
    We love what we've got —
Unabashed by some shameless rhymed plug

So don't judge a mutt by its mug —
This mugster gives heartstrings a tug
    You see him, you take him,
    You lift him and make him
As snug as a pug in a hug

The pug is living proof that God has a sense of humor.

— Margot Kaufman

iGNORANCE oF THE PAW iS NO EXCUSE

Does the passage of these laws by city councils and state legislatures mean that they had satisfactorily addressed all the more important issues? That they were ignoring them? That they have too much time on their hands?

It must have been fun to be part of those history-making discussions.

But vodka chasers are fine . . .

It is illegal to give a dog whiskey.

— Illinois state law

But Pitbulls are more than welcome . . .

It is illegal to take a French Poodle to the opera.

— Chicago, Illinois

Owners must signal them at the 14-minute mark . . .

It is illegal for dogs to bark for more than fifteen minutes.

— Northbrook, Illinois

But OK for domesticated animals not kept as pets?

It is illegal for anyone to give lighted cigars to dogs, cats, and other domesticated animals kept as pets.

— Zion, Illinois

Even good-smelly?

No person may keep a smelly dog.

— Galesburg, Illinois

Be sure to flip off the switch . . .

Dogs may not bark after 6:00 p.m.

— Little Rock, Arkansas

Imagine the sounds at 7:59 p.m. and 6:01 a.m. . . .

Dogs are not allowed to bark or howl between 8:00 p.m. and 6:00 a.m.

— Collingswood, New Jersey

But trucks are fine . . .

Dogs may not molest cars.

— Ft. Thomas, Kentucky

How about between women and men? . . .

In Barber, fights between cats and dogs are prohibited.

— Barber, North Carolina

Because if they do, they'll both get stuck up there and you'll have to call the fire department . . .

Cats are not permitted to chase dogs up telephone poles.

— International Falls, Minnesota

Because the squirrels are busy lobbying legislators . . .

Dogs are not allowed to worry squirrels in the public park next to the capitol.

— Madison, Wisconsin

They should just stuff their feelings . . .

Dogs may not act viciously, including excessively barking, growling, or acting in a menacing manner.

— Foxport, Wisconsin

A cop's bark is worse . . .

A police officer may bite a dog to quiet him, as long as it's in the line of duty.

— Paulding, Ohio

But Marysville removed its parking meters years ago . . .

It is illegal for a dog to urinate on a parking meter.

— Marysville, Ohio

But what if dogs make one first? . . .

People who make "ugly faces" at dogs may be fined and/or jailed.

— Some areas of Oklahoma

Apparently the First Amendment does not protect dogs' right to peacefully assemble . . .

Dogs must have a permit signed by the mayor in order to congregate in groups of three or more on private property.

— Oklahoma

This problem was serious enough to require a law? . . .

No one may tie their pet dog to the roof of a car.

— Anchorage, Alaska

Please use the yard around the public library . . .

Animals are not permitted to mate within 500 yards of a tavern, school, or place of worship.

— Some areas of California

Props to the prankster pol who put this parlance past . . .

No dog shall be in a public place without its master on a leash.

[And the dog had better pick up after its master!]

— Belvedere, California

Even with a permit, wouldn't it be pretty hard for these two species to mate? . . .

Cats and dogs are not allowed to mate without a permit.

— Ventura County, California

This gives dogs enough time to relocate. . .

The dog catcher must notify dogs of impounding by posting, for three consecutive days, a notice on a tree in the city park and along a public road running through said park.

— Denver, Colorado

Because they're clearly punks . . .

Any dogs bearing tattoos must be reported to the police.

— Connecticut

They'll just have to go out of state and pay costlier tuition . . .

It is illegal to educate dogs.

— Hartford, Connecticut

And humans may not talk after 10:00 . . .

Dogs are not allowed to bark after 6:00 p.m.

— Little Rock, Arkansas

Because if you give them too much rope . . .

Dog leashes may not be over eight feet in length.

— Waterboro, Maine

You wouldn't want to set a bad example for your dog . . .

Couples are not allowed to make out, or even hold hands, while walking a dog on a leash.

— New Castle, Delaware

Their owners are expected to do it for them . . .

Dogs are not allowed to cry.

— Wanessa, New Jersey

DOGS VS. KIDS

Why dogs are better than kids

- They eat less

- They don't ask for money

- They don't ask "Why?"

- They're easier to train

- They can be ready to leave the house in one second

- They'll always think you're smart

- They love naps

- They don't lie

- They're happy without video games and cell phones

- They aren't embarrassed to be seen with you

- They usually come when called

- They don't care if the peas touch the mashed potatoes

- They'll never drive your car

- They don't hang out with druggy friends

- They don't smoke or drink

- They don't want the latest fashions, or any fashions

- They can be housebroken in 3 months

- If they get pregnant, you can sell the pups

- No college

— Unknown

We've begun to long for the pitter-patter of little feet — so we bought a dog. Well, it's cheaper, and you get more feet.

— Rita Rudner

DOGS VS. MEN

The more I know about men the more I like dogs.

— Gloria Allred

I've seen a look in dogs' eyes, a quickly vanishing look of amazed contempt, and I am convinced that basically dogs think humans are nuts.

— John Steinbeck

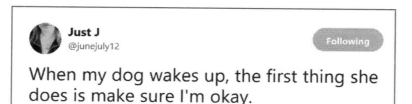

Just J
@junejuly12

Following

When my dog wakes up, the first thing she does is make sure I'm okay.

Men could learn from this.

How are dogs and men the same?

- Both take up too much space on the bed

- Both have an irrational fear of the vacuum

- Both are threatened by their own kind

- Both mark their territory

- Neither tells you what's bothering them

- The smaller ones tend to be more nervous

- Both have an inordinate fascination with women's crotches

- Neither does the dishes

- Both pass gas shamelessly

- Neither of them notice when you get a haircut

- Both like to play, especially dominance games

- Both would prefer to eat and sleep all day

- Neither understands what you see in cats

— Unknown

How are dogs better than men?

- Dogs miss you when you're gone

- Dogs don't mind being affectionate in public

- Dogs mean it when they kiss you

- Dogs look at your eyes, not your chest, when you talk to them

- Dogs know when they've done something wrong

- Dogs don't criticize your friends

- Dogs are nice to your relatives

- Dogs aren't threatened by your intelligence or higher income

- You can train a dog

- Dogs are easy to buy for

- Dogs don't play games with you — except fetch

- Dogs never laugh at how you throw

- You'll never be suspicious of your dog's dreams

- Dogs understand what "no" means

- Dogs understand if some of their friends can't come inside

- Middle-aged dogs won't leave you for someone younger

- Dogs are color blind

- Dogs don't brag about whom they've slept with

- Dogs aren't hung up about your prior romances

- Your dog would rather be with you than watch sports on TV

- Dogs are happy to go with you for a walk

- Dogs don't care what you look like or how much weight you've gained

- Dogs don't care how you dress

- Dogs don't mind if you do all the driving, and they won't criticize if you take a wrong turn

- Dogs think you're a culinary genius

— Unknown

Only my dogs will not betray me.

— Maria Callas

How are men better than dogs?

- Men have only two feet that track in mud

- Men can buy you presents

- Men don't have to play with every man they see when you take them around the block

- Dogs have dog breath all the time

- Men fix stuff

- Men don't shed (quite) as much

- It's more fun to dry off a wet man

- But that's about it

— Unknown

I never married because there was no need. I have three pets at home who answer the same purpose as a husband. I have a dog that growls every morning, a parrot that swears all afternoon, and a cat that comes home late every night.

— Marie Corelli

NEW RULE — If you're one of the one-in-three married women who say your pet is a better listener than your husband, you talk too much. And I have some bad news for you: Your dog's not listening, either — he's waiting for food to fall out of your mouth.

— Bill Maher

I just got a new dog, Sammy. He's my fourth beagle. I get about 14 or 15 years out of a beagle. I've been married three times and I never get more than ten years out of a husband. I get a lot more mileage out of a beagle than a husband, and if the dogs want to go out and run around, I can have 'em neutered.

— Meg Maly

Dogs have never hurt me. Only men have.

— Marilyn Monroe

The best thing about a man is his dog.

— French proverb

Some of my best leading men have been dogs and horses.

— Elizabeth Taylor

I hate when women compare men to dogs. Men are not dogs. Dogs are loyal. I've never found any strange panties in my dog's house.

— Wanda Sykes

When a man's dog turns against him it is time for a wife to pack her trunk and go home to mama.

— Mark Twain

The more I see of men the more I like dogs.

— Madame de Stael

DOGS ARE BETTER THAN PEOPLE

Who do people feel more empathy toward? Other people? Or dogs?

The correct answer, according to some research studies, is dogs.
Apparently many people feel dogs are better than people.

Our Quippery contributors tend to agree.

The average dog is a nicer person than the average person.

— Andy Rooney

Dogs are my favorite people.

— Richard Dean Anderson

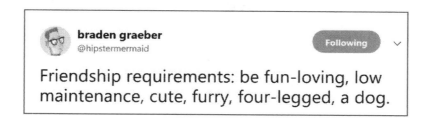

They are better than human beings, because they know but do not tell.

— Emily Dickinson

It's just the most amazing thing to love a dog, isn't it? It makes our relationships with people seem as boring as a bowl of oatmeal.

— John Grogan, *Marley and Me: Life and Love With the World's Worst Dog*

I love a dog. He does nothing for political reasons.

— Will Rogers

from Jerome K. Jerome

Yet, in general, I like cats and dogs very much indeed. What jolly chaps they are! They are much superior to human beings as companions. They do not quarrel or argue with you. They never talk about themselves, but listen to you while you talk about yourself, and keep up an appearance of being interested in the conversation. They never make stupid remarks. They never observe to Miss Brown across a dinner-table, that they always understood she was very sweet on Mr. Jones (who has just married Miss Robinson). They never mistake your wife's cousin for her husband, and fancy that you are the father-in-law. And they never ask a young author with fourteen tragedies, sixteen comedies, seven farces, and a couple of burlesques in his desk, why he doesn't write a play.

They never say unkind things. They never tell us of our faults, "merely for our own good." They do not, at inconvenient moments, mildly remind us of our past follies and mistakes. They do not say, "Oh yes, a lot of use you are, if you are ever really wanted" — sarcastic-like. They never inform us, like our inamoratas sometimes do, that we are not nearly so nice as we used to be. We are always the same to them.

They are always glad to see us. They are with us in all our humours. They are merry when we are glad, sober when we feel solemn, sad when we are sorrowful.

"Hulloa! happy, and want a lark! Right you are; I'm your man. Here I am, frisking round you, leaping, barking, pirouetting, ready for any amount of fun and mischief. Look at my eyes, if you doubt me. What shall it be? A romp in the drawing-room, and never mind the furniture, or a scamper in the fresh, cool air, a scud across the fields, and down the hill, and won't we let old Gaffer Goggles's geese know what time o'day it is, neither. Whoop! come along."

And when we bury our face in our hands and wish we had never been born, they don't sit up very straight, and observe that we have brought it all upon ourselves. They don't even hope it will be a warning to us. But they come up softly; and shove their heads against us. If it is a cat, she stands on your shoulder, rumples your hair and says, "Lor', I am sorry for you, old man," as plain as words can speak; and if it is a dog, he looks up at you with his big, true eyes, and says with them, "Well, you've always got me, you know. We'll go through the world together, and always stand by each other, won't we?"

He is very imprudent, a dog is. He never makes it his business to inquire whether you are in the right or in the wrong, never bothers as to whether you are going up or down upon life's ladder, never asks whether you are rich or poor, silly or wise, sinner or saint. You are his pal. That is enough for him, and, come luck or misfortune, good repute or bad, honour or shame, he is going to stick to you, to comfort you, guard you, give his life for you, if need be — foolish, brainless, soulless dog!

— "On Cats and Dogs," *The Idle Thoughts of an Idle Fellow* (1890)

Man is troubled by what might be called the Dog Wish, a strange and involved compulsion to be as happy and carefree as a dog.

— James Thurber

A dog is not almost human, and I know of no greater insult to the canine race than to describe it as such.

— John Holmes

To err is human, to forgive, canine.

— Anonymous

Baseball Chickie!
@baseballchickie

Following

Friend: You should try to make new friends.
Me: No thank you......Wait, are they dogs?
F: No, human friends.
M: No thank you.

from The Onion

NEWS IN BRIEF

Woman With Six Dogs Resents Non-Dogs

ALBANY, CA — Bay Area resident Emily Dobbyns, owner of two wire-haired fox terriers, two shih tzus, one Maltese, and a pug, revealed yesterday that she resents all non-canine life forms. "My family and coworkers and friends are so hard to get along with," Dobbyns said, petting her pug Skipper. "They're so opinionated, and they let their egos complicate everything." Dobbyns added that her little Skipperdoodle would never expect her to drive 22 miles to a birthday party at a restaurant she doesn't even like.

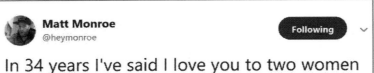

Who is the more advanced being — humans or dogs?

- If you can live without caffeine . . .

- If you can be cheerful, ignoring aches and pains . . .

- If you can resist complaining . . .

- If you can eat the same food every day and be grateful for it . . .

- If you can understand when your loved ones are too busy to give you time . . .

- If you can overlook it when those you love take it out on you when, through no fault of yours, something goes wrong . . .

- If you can take criticism and blame without resentment . . .

- If you can ignore friends' limited education and never correct them . . .

- If you can resist treating a rich friend better than a poor friend . . .

- If you can face the world without lies and deceit . . .

- If you can conquer tension without medical help. . .

- If you can relax without liquor . . .

- If you can sleep without the aid of drugs . . .

- If you can honestly say that deep in your heart you have no prejudice against creed, color, religion, gender preference, or politics . . .

. . . then you have *almost* reached the same level of spiritual development as your dog.

Sign on a front door:

"If our dog doesn't like you, we probably won't either."

The dog has seldom been successful in pulling man up to its level of sagacity, but man has frequently dragged the dog down to his.

— James Thurber

30 Reasons Why Dogs Are Better Than Humans

Gabrielle Lintz

Humans don't have a ruff life, but being a dog would be pretty paw-some.

At family gatherings, I'm pretty sure people are more interested in petting the dog than saying hi to you. Ain't that the truth? They're cute, they're fluffy, and they're friendly; traits – for the most part – that most humans do not possess. Dogs are the life of any party, and let's be honest, they're probably more adored than you in your household. Their cheerful greetings to you at the door after a long day can instantly make you smile and feel so at home and comfortable. I wish everyone was as loving and easygoing as dogs are.

Here are some valid reasons why dogs are *so* much better than humans.

1. They're happier than humans.

2. Eat. Sleep. Play. Repeat. (I'd always be happy, too.)

3. Dogs can't screw up as a best friend. They are the ultimate companion.

4. Pups are always willing to cuddle. Who needs a significant other when you have a puppy?

5. They look good in collars, unlike children.

6. Dogs listen to your problems, and they don't interrupt.

7. If they don't like you, they bite you. No one likes passive aggressive humans anyways.

8. Dogs are protective and extremely alert. They have much better senses than people do.

9. Even if they smell, they'll still be loved.

10. And even if they're ugly, they're still cute.

11. Did I mention they can't talk?

12. They don't judge you.

13. They're the ultimate wingman/woman. Nothing says, "I'm datable" like having a cute dog by your side.

14. "They can lick their own butts." — Anonymous guy I asked regarding the topic.

15. Dogs always show unconditional love.

16. They're always loyal to you. It's not like they can make plans without you. . . .

17. They're not picky where they poop or pee . . . public restrooms aren't always our favorite. Imagine the grass?

18. Dogs don't spend money on food, their owners do it for them.

19. Dogs are all selfless. Not all people are.

20. You can name them funnier names than the basic "Ashley" or "John." Try "Chubby" and "Banjo," which are so much cooler.

21. They don't have to bathe every single day.

22. Or brush their hair.

23. Or brush their teeth.

24. Sounds gross, but dogs are just so carefree.

25. They don't have to drive anywhere. Personal chauffeurs for life.

26. People voluntarily play with their hair all the time.

27. Their biggest trouble is having an itch.

28. People only stay mad at dogs for like two minutes.

29. Dogs don't have to work or have any responsibilities.

30. Oh, and best of all, dogs don't have college tuition.

The dog has got more fun out of Man than Man has got out of the dog, for the clearly demonstrable reason that Man is the more laughable of the two animals.

— James Thurber

Do not make the mistake of treating your dogs like humans or they will treat you like dogs.

— Martha Scott

Dogs' lives are too short. Their only fault, really.

— Agnes Sligh Turnbull

DOCTORING DOGS

Taking the Zip out of Zippy

I regularly get letters from irate MacNeil-Lehrer-watching readers who ask: "With all the serious problems facing the world, how come you write about your dogs?" To which I answer: Because I don't know anything about *your* dogs. Also — you can call me an idealist if you want, but this is my opinion — by writing about my dogs, I believe that I can bring my readers — rich and poor, young and old, intelligent and "lite"-beer drinking — to a greater awareness of, and appreciation for, my dogs. I want my dogs to someday be at least as famous as Loni Anderson. I want them to receive lucrative offers for major motion pictures based on their True Life Adventures.

This week, for example, our adventure is entitled:

ZIPPY AND EARNEST GET OPERATED ON

This adventure began when Zippy went through puberty, a biological process that a small dog goes through in less time than it takes you to throw away your Third Class mail. One minute Zippy was a cute little-boy puppy, scampering about the house playfully causing permanent damage to furniture that is not yet fully paid for; and the next minute he was: A Man. When the new, mature version of Zippy sauntered into a room, you could almost hear the great blues musician Muddy Waters in the background, growling:

I'm a MAN

(harmonica part)

Yes I AM

(harmonica part)

A FULL-GROWN man.

Of course in Zippy's case, "full-grown" means "the size of a Hostess Sno-Ball, yet somehow less impressive." But in his own mind, Zippy was a major stud muffin, a hunk of burnin' love, a small-caliber but high-velocity Projectile of Passion fired from the Saturday Night Special of Sex. And his target was: Earnest.

Earnest is a female dog, but she was not the ideal choice for Zippy, because all of her remotely suspicious organs had been surgically removed several years ago. Since that time she has not appeared to be even dimly aware of sex, or much of anything else. Her lone hobby, besides eating, is barking violently at nothing. Also she is quite large; when she's standing up, Zippy can run directly under her with an easy six inches of clearance. So at first we were highly amused when he started putting The Moves on her. It was like watching Tommy Tadpole hit on the Queen Mary.

But shortly the novelty wore off and we started feeling sorry for Ernest, who spent the entire day staring glumly off into dog hyperspace while this tireless yarn-ball-sized Lust Machine kept leaping up on her, sometimes getting as high as mid-shin, and emitting these presumably seductive high-pitched yips ("What's your sign? What's your sign?"). So we decided it was time to have the veterinarian turn the volume knob of desire way down on the stereo system of Zippy's manhood. If you get my drift.

The next morning Earnest was limping, so we decided to take both dogs to the vet. They bounded enthusiastically into the car, of course; dogs feel very strongly that they should always go with you in the car, in case the need should arise for them to bark violently at nothing right in your ear. When we got to the veterinarian's office they realized they had been tricked and went into Full Reverse Thrust, but fortunately the floor material there is slippery enough to luge on. So when we last saw Zippy and Earnest that morning, they were being towed, all eight legs scrabbling in a wild, backward, futile blur, into: the Back Room.

When we picked them up that night, they were a pair of hurtin' cowpokes. Earnest, who had a growth removed, was limping badly, plus we had to put a plastic bag on her leg so she wouldn't lick her stitches off. And Zippy, to keep him from getting at *his* stitches, was wearing a large and very comical round plastic collar that looked liked a satellite dish with Zippy's head sticking out the middle. He had a lot of trouble getting around, because his collar kept hitting things, such as the ground.

For the next week, if you came to our front door, here's what happened: You heard the loud barking of two dogs going into Red Alert mode, but you did not see any immediate dogs. Instead you heard a lot of bumping and clunking, which turned out to be the sound of a large dog limping frantically toward you but suffering a major traction loss on every fourth step because of a plastic bag, combined with the sound of a very small dog trying desperately to keep up but bonking his collar into furniture, doorways, etc. And then, finally, skidding around the corner, still barking, there appeared the dynamite duo: Bagfoot and Satellite Head.

During this week we were not the least bit worried about burglars, because if anyone had tried to break into our house, we would have found him the next morning, lying in a puddle of his own drool. Dead from laughter.

— *Dave Barry Talks Back*

Max Dylan Ahhhh!-sh
@mynameisntdave

Following

If you want your dog to take a pill:

1. Get a piece of cheese

2. Eat the cheese for energy

3. Get ready to wrestle your dog

from The Onion

NEWS IN BRIEF

Man Not Sure What To Do About Vet's Request For Dog-Urine Sample

MISSOULA, MT — Dog owner Darryl Burkhard, 36, said Tuesday that he is unsure how to fulfill his veterinarian's orders to extract a urine sample from ailing cocker spaniel Sneakers. "The vet just casually asked me to bring in a sample, like I'd automatically know how to do that," Burkhard said. "Do I take Sneakers for a walk and then stick a cup under him at just the right moment? Or do I, like, fasten a cup to his genitals with a belt and wait for him to eventually go? Either way, I'm probably looking at some sort of really unpleasant dog-piss-related situation."

DOG BARKS

A dog's bark is worse than its bite.

What's that supposed to mean? A dog bite can might puncture your skin but a dog's bark can break your collarbone?

Actually, a woman in Philadelphia got ten days in jail because her five barking dogs were "torturing the neighbors." A North Seattle woman was sued by her neighbor for her dog's "raucously, wildly bellowing, howling, and explosively barking," which caused him "profound emotional distress." We can imagine that.

Dogs bark because they're trying to communicate something. But what is that something? They don't always say.

When I yell at my dog to stop barking, I wonder if he's like, "This is awesome! We are barking together!"

— Unknown

from Dave Barry

During this difficult time [moving to a new house], we have received a large mound of assistance from our two dogs. Using their keen, nearly asphalt-level intelligence, they have sensed that something important is happening and have decided that their vital contribution will be to kill anybody who comes near our house. This means they have to spend a lot of time shut away in my office, barking. They've reached the point where they automatically start barking as soon as we shut them in there, whether or not there's anybody to bark at yet. It's their job, barking in my office. Somebody has to do it! They produce approximately one bark apiece every two seconds, so if I leave them in there for, say, 45 minutes, then open the door, I get knocked several feet backward by the escaping force of 2,700 accumulated barks.

— *Dave Barry Talks Back*

JustSomeFool
@just1fool

Following

I always wonder if my dog is dreaming about defending my honor when he barks in his sleep.

from The Onion

NEWS IN BRIEF

Dog Chastised For Acting Like Dog

SACRAMENTO, CA — Obeying the instincts bred into him by millions of years of evolution, Shiner, a 2-year-old golden retriever, incurred his owner's wrath Monday by acting like a dog. "Stop barking at that damn squirrel!" Terri Solanis shouted at the dog. "Can't you sit still for five minutes?" Solanis has previously scolded Shiner for sniffing feces encountered on the sidewalk, licking his own groin, and wolfing down his food.

When a child is locked in the bathroom with water running and he says he's doing nothing but the dog is barking, call 911.

— Erma Bombeck

With my dog I don't get no respect. He keeps barking at the front door. He doesn't want to go out. He wants me to leave.

— Rodney Dangerfield

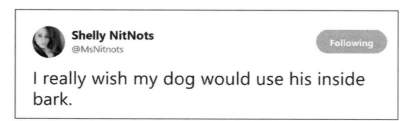

Shelly NitNots
@MsNitnots

Following

I really wish my dog would use his inside bark.

I once undertook on behalf of a friend to smuggle a small dog through the customs. I was of ample proportions, and managed to conceal the little dog upon my person. All went well until my bosom barked.

— Mrs. Patrick Campbell (English actress)

from The Onion

NEWS IN BRIEF

Family Dog Barking At Evil

MEDFORD, OR — Spraggles, the Reid family's terrier, was barking at evil again Monday, his canine instincts detecting the presence of an unseen sinister force. "What on Earth is he carrying on about?" asked owner Ed Reid, watching Spraggles bark at a hall closet. "There's nothing in that closet but Grandma's old wedding gown and a hammer." Spraggles then headed to the backyard to bark at more evil, this time in the form of a newspaper page swirling in the wind.

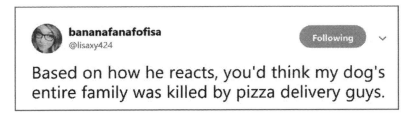

bananafanafofisa
@lisaxy424
Following ⌄

Based on how he reacts, you'd think my dog's entire family was killed by pizza delivery guys.

from Clickhole

5 Explorers Who Saw the Americas Before Columbus but Turned Back Because of a Dog Barking Along the Shore

We all know the history: In 1492, Christopher Columbus became the first explorer to arrive in the Americas, right? Wrong. Here are five explorers who saw the Americas with their own eyes long before Columbus, but turned back and went home because of a dog barking along the shore.

1. Leif Erikson

One of the most overlooked explorers in history, Leif Erikson led the Vikings on numerous sea voyages in search of the unknown. In 1000 A.D., he and his crew landed in the Americas, only to find a huge dog barking right there on the shore. Erikson and his crew spent hours kind of sailing up and down the shoreline looking for an open place to dock, but the dog just trotted alongside them, barking at them the entire time. It was big as hell and didn't have a collar on or anything, so eventually Leif Erikson and his crew had no choice but to turn around and go back to Iceland.

2. Zheng He

Zheng He's legacy as an explorer lives on as one of the most daring and relentless in history. His most successful voyage came in the 13th century when he sailed right up to the shores of today's San Diego, where an absolute goliath of a Greyhound, or maybe a Doberman, was barking like a maniac onshore. Zheng had his crew collect up as much salt pork as they could find on the ship and toss it to the dog as an olive branch, but the dog just wolfed it down crazy-fast then started barking even louder. Finally, Zheng decided to just leave the Americas alone.

3. Henry Sinclair

Henry Sinclair, one of Scotland's highest-ranking political figures in the late 12th century in his role as Admiral of the Seas, departed for the New World in 1394. In 1399, he and his crew finally laid eyes on the Americas, along with a big-ass Rottweiler totally losing its mind on the beach. Sinclair sent a few sailors in a smaller boat to try to calm the dog down, but the dog was going completely apeshit the closer they got, so they decided to just bail on the whole thing.

4. Abu Bakr II

From about a mile off of the coast of Virginia during his early 12th-century voyage, African explorer Abu Bakr's lookout shouted from the crow's nest that there was a dog on the beach and that he had "gotten bit pretty bad by a dog once." The captain immediately turned the fleet around and went home.

5. Prince Madoc

When Prince Madoc set out to discover the new continent in 1171, he had no way of knowing that he'd be lucky enough to find it, and unlucky enough to find a barking dog right where he was trying to dock. According to Madoc's private records, the dog on shore "had to be a Siberian Husky or, like, a German Shepherd, and looked ready to take someone's face off." Madoc circled around the area a few times to see if the dog would think they were leaving for good, but every time he came back, the dog would hop up from lying on its back and start barking again. After yelling "Sit!" a few times at the dog, Madoc gave up and returned to Wales, opening the door for Christopher Columbus to settle the Americas hundreds of years later and get all the credit.

A dog syllogism

All trees have bark.
All dogs bark.
Therefore, all dogs are trees.

from The Onion

NEWS IN BRIEF

Nation's Dogs Vow To Keep Their Shit Together During 4th Of July Fireworks

WASHINGTON — Admitting that their behavior in previous years had left them embarrassed and ashamed, the nation's dogs announced Thursday that they intend on keeping their shit together during this year's Fourth of July fireworks displays. "Though we recognize we have not always demonstrated the most poise and self-control on this particular holiday, we want to assure everyone that this will finally be the year we don't completely lose it and freak out upon hearing the booming of distant fireworks," said Duchess, a 6-year-old cocker spaniel, adding that the country's 80 million dogs aim to avoid cowering under the coffee table or uncontrollably urinating on the kitchen floor in a moment of pure panic after neighbors light off firecrackers or bottle rockets. "We've been preparing for the past few months, and we think we'll finally be able to maintain our composure this time around. We can't promise that we won't whimper a little or try to jump up and sit next to you on the couch, but we're definitely not going to sprint in circles around the living room or howl continuously until the noises stop." The nation's dogs concluded by acknowledging they could not guarantee that they won't go completely apeshit the next time the doorbell rings.

DOG BITES

When a dog bites a man, that is not news, but when a man bites a dog, that is news.

— Charles Anderson Dana, "What Is News?", *The New York Sun*

I loathe people who keep dogs. They are cowards who haven't got the guts to bite people themselves.

— August Strindberg

Albert Einstein had a fox terrier he named Chico Marx, after one of the famous Marx Brothers (the one who never spoke). "The dog is very smart," Einstein said. "He feels sorry for me because I receive so much mail. That's why he tries to bite the mailman."

Keep running after a dog and he will never bite you.

— Francois Rabelais

If you pick up a starving dog and make him prosperous, he will not bite you; that is the principal difference between a dog and a man.

— Mark Twain

DOG COMMUNICADO

Dogs have things they want to say. Every dog owner knows that.

They bark, howl, growl, whimper, simper, whine, huff, grunt, yip, yelp, and more. They also communicate through tail wagging, facial expressions, body language, and relieving themselves. In recent years, many dogs have taken to Facebook, but now, concerned about privacy issues and the company's business model, they're migrating to Snapchat and Instagram.

My dog winks at me sometimes. And I always wink back just in case it's some kind of code.

— Unknown

Do you talk to your dog? I think that is healthy. After all, your dog understands you. If you talk to your cat, I think you should seek professional help. Talking to your dog is therapeutic. Your dog will listen to you intently.

— Al Batt

They never talk about themselves but listen to you while you talk about yourself, and keep up an appearance of being interested in the conversation.

— Jerome K. Jerome

I hope science never figures out how to make dogs talk. If my dog ever learns to talk, everyone will know my deepest darkest secrets in exchange for a slice of cheese or something.

— Unknown

Maybe dogs really can talk, but they don't, and instead act stupid so they can infiltrate as many households as possible before taking over the world.

— Unknown

Many of us have to spell words such as "out," "cookie," and "bath" when conversing with other people, lest we unnecessarily excite our pets. And even then they often understand. I've actually had clients who resorted to using a second language around their dogs, but after a while their perceptive pooches caught on. Who says dogs don't understand us?

— Warren Eckstein

"Hey, this isn't the girl who stayed the night last night, she smells different" — cheaters everywhere would have a tough time if they had a dog that could talk.

— Unknown

A dog's dictionary

BATH — This is a process by which the humans drench the floor, walls and themselves. You can help by shaking vigorously and frequently.

BICYCLES — Two-wheeled exercise machines, invented for dogs to control body fat. To get maximum aerobic benefit, you must hide behind a bush and dash out, bark loudly, and run alongside for a few yards; the person then swerves and falls into the bushes.

BUMP — The best way to get your human's attention when they are drinking a fresh cup of coffee or tea.

DEAFNESS — This is a malady which affects dogs when their person wants them in and they want to stay out. Symptoms include staring blankly at the person, then running in the opposite direction, or lying down.

DOG BED — Any soft, clean surface, such as the white bedspread in the guest room or the newly upholstered couch in the living room.

DROOL — What you do when your persons have food and you don't. To do this properly you must sit as close as you can and look sad and let the drool fall to the floor or better yet, on their laps.

GARBAGE CAN — A container which your neighbors put out once a week to test your ingenuity. You must stand on your hind legs and try to push the lid off with your nose. If you do it right you are rewarded with margarine wrappers to shred, beef bones to consume, and moldy crusts of bread.

LEASH — A strap which attaches to your collar, enabling you to lead your person where you want him or her to go.

LOVE — A feeling of intense affection, given freely and without restriction. The best way you can show your love is to wag your tail. If you're lucky, a human will love you in return.

SNIFF — A social custom to use when you greet other dogs. Place your nose as close as you can to the other dog's rear end and inhale deeply, repeat several times, or until your person makes you stop. Can also be done with human crotches.

SOFAS — Are to dogs like napkins are to people. After eating it is polite to run up and down the front of the sofa and wipe your whiskers clean.

THUNDER — This is a signal that the world is coming to an end. Humans remain amazingly calm during thunderstorms, so it is necessary to warn them of the danger by trembling uncontrollably, panting, rolling your eyes wildly, and following at their heels.

WASTEBASKET — This is a dog toy filled with paper, envelopes, and old candy wrappers. When you get bored, turn over the basket and strew the papers all over the house until your person comes home.

— Unknown

My dog, she looks at me sometimes with that look, and I think maybe deep down inside she must know exactly how I feel. But then maybe she just wants the food off my plate.

— Unknown

The reason a dog has so many friends is that he wags his tail instead of his tongue.

— Unknown

When a dog wags her tail and barks at the same time, how do you know which end to believe?

— Character Tom Dobbs, in *"Man of the Year"* (2006), screenplay by Barry Levinson

The other day a dog peed on me. A bad sign.

— H.L. Mencken

If dogs could talk, it would take a lot of the fun out of owning one.

— Andy Rooney

A DOG'S LOVE

Can you measure the love humans and dogs have for each other?

Researchers have tried. They find that when pet owners look into their dogs' eyes, there's a 130% spike in oxytocin, "the cuddle hormone." And in dogs? Oxytocin goes through the roof — a 300% spike. "Dogs," one of the researchers said, "have hijacked the human bonding system."

A dog is the only thing on earth that loves you more than you love yourself.

— Josh Billings

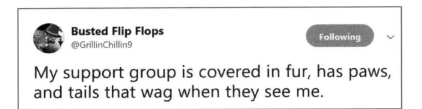

It's not until you're an adult you appreciate how awesome a dog is. Your dreams start dying, somebody cheats on you, bankers fuck up your 401k, you know? Then you come home and that dog's looking at you and he's like, "Dude, you're awesome!" It's like, "No, dude you . . . you are fucking awesome!"

— Bill Burr

You really have to be some kind of a creep for a dog to reject you.

— Joe Garagiola

The dog has no ambition, no self-interest, no desire for vengeance, no fear other than that of displeasing.

— Count of Buffon

Kimtopher
@kimtopher22

Following

I'm having an affair.

Don't know her name, we meet on her terms. She jumps on the fence to kiss me as I walk by her house.

I love dogs.

We give dogs time we can spare, space we can spare and love we can spare. And in return, dogs give us their all. It's the best deal man has ever made.

— Margery Facklam

Robert Knop
@FatherWithTwins

Following

*I walk through door
My dogs: I LOVE YOU I LOVE YOU I LOVE YOU
*random stranger walks through door
My dogs: I LOVE YOU I LOVE YOU I LOVE YOU

The reason I love my dog so much is because when I come home, he's the only one in the world who treats me like I'm The Beatles.

— Bill Maher

Not Carnegie, Vanderbilt and Astor together could have raised money enough to buy a quarter share in my little dog.

— Ernest Thompson Seton

To his dog, every man is Napoleon; hence the constant popularity of dogs.

— Aldous Huxley

from Dave Barry

6:00 A.M. — Alarm goes off.

6:10, 6:20, 6:30, 6:40, 6:50 A.M. — Alarm goes off.

7:00 A.M. — Wake up and mentally review Plan of Action for accomplishing Today's Target Tasks.

7:10 A.M. — Alarm goes off.

7:11 A.M. — Open bedroom door and greet dogs.
(NOTE: I always allow at least then minutes for this, because dogs have the same IQ as artichokes, and thus when they see me close the door at night — even though they've seen me do this approximately 1,300 times — they are certain they'll never see me again, and consequently they give me an insanely joyful welcome comparable to the one given the Allied forces when they liberated Paris, the difference being that the Parisians were slightly less likely, in their enthusiasm, to pee on your feet.)

. . . .

6:39 P.M. — Arrive home to insanely joyful greeting from dogs, who, believing themselves abandoned forever, spent entire day throwing up in despair.

— *Dave Barry Turns 40*

The great pleasure of a dog is that you make a fool of yourself with him and not only will he not scold you, but he will make a fool of himself, too.

— Samuel Butler

No one appreciates the very special genius of your conversation as the dog does.

— Christopher Morley

When you leave them in the morning, they stick their nose in the door crack and stand there like a portrait until you turn the key eight hours later.

— Erma Bombeck

Some of our greatest historical and artistic treasures we place with curators in museums; others we take for walks.

— Roger Caras, *A Celebration of Dogs*

Dog owner's prayer:
"Lord, let me be the kind of person my dog thinks I am."
— Unknown

Man is a dog's idea of what God should be.

— Holbrook Jackson

Reality checks

If your dog thinks you're the greatest person in the world, don't seek a second opinion.

— Jim Fiebig

Know yourself. Don't accept your dog's admiration as conclusive evidence that you are wonderful.

— Ann Landers

A DOG'S RESUMÉ

CAPTAIN JACK

American Mixed Breed Family Dog

Work Experience

Caine Household, The Dog   **2016-Present**

- Protect the family from squirrels real and imagined

- Ensure that humans receive a minimum level of daily physical exercise

- Greeter

- Wrestle with the man when he comes home from work

- Twice daily squirrel hunts

- Light custodial work cleaning up spilled food

- Amateur therapy dog

Lost Dog & Cat Rescue Foundation, Hard Luck Case 2015-2016

- Toured area Petsmart locations interviewing prospective owners

West Virginia High Kill Animal Shelter, Inmate #3294   2014

- Sentence lifted upon successful appeal

Education

The Hoard Hound Doggy Daycare   2013

- Expelled for excessively rough play

Professional Skills and Certifications

- Licensed with the City of Westchester and the Perro Condo Association

- Experienced with both extendable leash and gentle leader

- Parlaying displays of affection into belly rubs

- Highly proficient at both "sit" and "shake" when properly motivated

- Neutered

- Shots up to date through December 2018

- Good boy

Achievements

- Territory marked in five states and the District of Columbia

- Squirrels apprehended and neutralized: 2

- Cicadas eaten: 1

- Went to the beach. Water tasted terrible.

- Consumed an entire raw steak obtained from the counter in under 30 seconds

- Once climbed a tree (in pursuit of a squirrel)

Desired Salary

- Pig ears to chicken skin

RANDOM DOG QUIPPERY

There is honor in being a dog.

— Aristotle

I took my dog for a walk, all the way from New York to Florida. I said to him "There now, you're done."

— Steven Wright

I was a dog in a past life. Really. I'll be walking down the street and dogs will do a sort of double take. Like, Hey, I know him.

— William H. Macy

Your dog will look at you when you are worth looking at.

— Sam Malatesta

Asking a working writer what he thinks about critics is like asking a lamp post how it feels about dogs.

— Christopher Hampton

If you get to thinking you're a person of some influence, try ordering somebody else's dog around.

— Will Rogers

A dog is one of the remaining reasons why some people can be persuaded to go for a walk.

— O.A. Battista

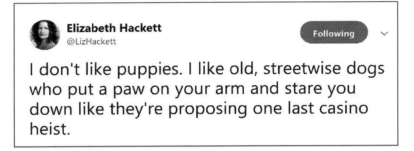

Home computers are being called upon to perform many new functions, including the consumption of homework formerly eaten by the dog.

— Doug Larson

I looked up my family tree and found three dogs using it.

— Rodney Dangerfield

Scratch a dog and you'll find a permanent job.

— Franklin P. Jones

Some days you're the dog; some days you're the hydrant.

— Unknown

Too bad Lassie didn't know how to ice skate, because then if she was in Holland on vacation in winter and someone said, "Lassie, go skate for help," she could do it.

— Jack Handey, *Deep Thoughts*

In dog years, I'm dead.

— Unknown

I spilled spot remover on my dog. He's gone now.

— Steven Wright

from Ellen DeGeneres

I try to save dogs and take them to shelters so that their owners can find them. It's because I have dogs, and I know I'd be devastated if either . . . damn, what are their names? Oh yeah . . . if either Bootsie or Lippy . . . no, not Lippy . . . Muffin. If either Bootsie or Muffin got lost . . . Bootsie is a beautiful Labrador retriever and Muffin is . . . I'm not exactly sure what Muffin is. When I got her at the shelter, they told me that she was part cocker spaniel and part terrier, but I don't think they knew. They were just making conversation. I think she's part . . . rodent. She's got hair like a possum and a snout like an anteater. But, don't get the wrong impression, she's very pretty. She's got off-beat good looks.

I'll see stray dogs wandering in front of houses and they look so sad. I just feel compelled to do something to rescue them. Sometimes it's hard because they're tied on a leash on someone's front lawn, so you've got to untie it. Or worse, they're behind a fence, so you need wire cutters (which I always have in my car) to get them out. "C'mon, girl. I'll rescue you and find your owners."

— *My Point . . . And I Do Have One*

You enter into a certain amount of madness when you marry a person with pets.

— Nora Ephron

I care not for a man's religion whose dog and cat are not the better for it.

— Abraham Lincoln

If your dog is fat, you aren't getting enough exercise.

— Unknown

Sooner or later we're all someone's dog.

— Terry Pratchett

Diplomacy is the art of saying "Nice doggie" until you can find a rock.

— Will Rogers

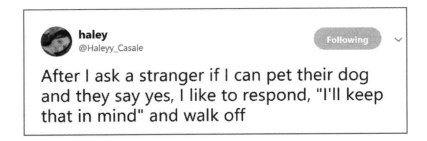

A dog is a dog except when he is facing you. Then he is Mr. Dog.

— Haitian farmer

Did you hear about the dyslexic agnostic insomniac who stays up all night wondering if there really is a Dog?

— Unknown

There are three faithful friends — an old wife, an old dog, and ready money.

— Ben Franklin

from Jerome K. Jerome

If you want to make love to the eldest daughter, or get the old man to lend you the garden roller, or the mother to subscribe to the Society for the Suppression of Solo-cornet Players in Theatrical Orchestras (it's a pity there isn't one, anyhow), you have to begin with the dog. You must gain its approbation before they will even listen to you, and if, as is highly probable, the animal, whose frank doggy nature has been warped by the unnatural treatment he has received, responds to your overtures of friendship by viciously snapping at you, your cause is lost forever.

— "On Cats and Dogs," *The Idle Thoughts of an Idle Fellow* (1890)

I went to an exclusive kennel club. It was very exclusive. There was a sign out front: "No Dogs Allowed."

— Phil Foster

Bring Your Dog to Work Day: Do dogs really need to see corporate life? Aren't they already used to sniffing butts?

— Jay Leno

He that lieth down with dogs, shall rise up with fleas.

— Ben Franklin

My advice to any diplomat who wants to have good press is to have two or three kids and a dog.

— Carl Rowan

It's tough to stay married. My wife kisses the dog on the lips, yet she won't drink from my glass.

— Rodney Dangerfield

Finding my dog's G-spot is taking way longer than I would care to admit.

— Daniel Tosh

DOG HEAVEN

The dog is a gentleman; I hope to go to his heaven, not man's.

— Mark Twain

If there are no dogs in heaven, then when I die, I want to go where they went.

— Will Rogers

If I have any beliefs about immortality, it is that certain dogs I have known will go to heaven, and very, very few persons.

— James Thurber

Heaven goes by favor. If it went by merit, you would stay out and your dog would go in.

— Mark Twain

You think those dogs will not be in heaven! I tell you they will be there long before any of us.

— Robert Louis Stevenson

If you don't mind throwing tennis balls for eternity, I do have an opening in doggie heaven.

— *Frank and Ernest* comic strip

WHAT CAN WE LEARN FROM DOGS?

So many get reformed through religion. I got reformed through dogs.

— Lina Basquette

Any woman who does not thoroughly enjoy tramping across the country on a clear frosty morning with a good gun and a pair of dogs does not know how to enjoy life.

— Annie Oakley

Isn't it wonderful how dogs can win friends and influence people without ever reading a book?

— E.C. McKenzie

from Merrill Markoe

What the Dogs Have Taught Me

Daily Routine

The day is divided into two important sections. *Mealtime*. And *everything else*.

I. Mealtime

1. Just because there does not seem to be anything *visible* around to eat certainly does not mean there is *nothing* around to eat. The act of staring at the underside of a table or chair on which someone else is eating sets in motion a chain of events that eventually results in food.

2. It goes without saying that you should carefully check the lower third of *any* space for edibles. Mouth-sized things which cannot be identified by sight or smell are considered gum.

3. When you actually receive a meal, submerge your head into it as you would a shower. *Never, ever* look up again until a minimum of at least fifteen minutes after the obvious food is gone. This is important. Just because your dish is empty does not mean that it is time to stop eating.

4. Remember that *all* food is potentially yours up until the time that it is actually swallowed by another. The lengthy path a piece of food will

take from a plate to a mouth via a hand is as good a time as any to stake your claim to it.

5.　When it comes to selecting an appropriate beverage, location and packaging mean *nothing*. There are *absolutely no exceptions* to this rule.

6.　If you really see something you want, and all your other attempts at getting it have failed, it is only right to grovel shamelessly. As a second tactic, stare intently at the object of your desire, allowing long gelatinous drools to leak like icicles from your lower lip.

II. Everything Else

1.　There are really only two important facial expressions to bother with: *complete overwhelming joy* and *nothing at all*.

2.　Any time that is not meal time is potentially nap time. The best time to take a nap is when you hear your name being called repeatedly. The best location for a nap is dead center of any street or driveway. The most relaxing position is on your side, all four limbs parallel.

3.　The most practical way to get dry is to shake violently near a fully clothed person. A second effective method is to stand on a light-colored piece of furniture.

4. *Personal Security*

   A. At the first hint of any irregular noise, run from room to room yelling loudly. If someone actually comes into the house, rush over to them whether you know them or not. Then kiss them so violently that they lose their balance or have to force you away physically.

   B. The greatest unacknowledged threat to life as we have come to know it is squirrels. No matter what you must do, make sure there are none in your yard.

5. *Recreation and Leisure*

   A. *Ball*: No matter where you find them, in a bed or in a bathtub, no matter how they are dressed or how they behave, there is no such thing as a person who does not want to play ball all the time. There are two equally amusing sets of rules you will want to know.

      a. *The common form*, in which you receive a thrown ball and return it.

      b. *The preferred form*, in which you receive a thrown ball and eat it.

   B. *Car*: As you know, any open car door is an invitation to get in. Once inside, your only goal is to try to get out.

6. *Health*

  A. In the event of a trip to the doctor, always be on your guard. If you are vaccinated, urinate on the physician.

Afterword

Since I have taken to sleeping under the bed, I have come to know tranquility I never imagined possible.

You never really know when it might be cookie time. And that's what the dogs have taught me.

— *What the Dogs Have Taught Me: And Other Amazing Things I've Learned*

A dog teaches a boy fidelity, perseverance, and to turn around three times before lying down.

— Robert Benchley

Things We Can Learn from a Dog

Joy Nordquist

1. Never pass up the opportunity to go for a joy ride.

2. Allow the experience of fresh air and the wind in your face to be pure ecstasy.

3. When loved ones come home, always run to greet them.

4. When it's in your best interest, always practice obedience.

5. Let others know when they've invaded your territory.

6. Take naps and always stretch before rising.

7. Run, romp and play daily.

8   Eat with gusto and enthusiasm.

9. Be loyal.

10. Never pretend to be something you're not.

11. If what you want lies buried, dig until you find it.

12. When someone is having a bad day, be silent, sit close by and nuzzle them gently.

13. Delight in the simple joy of a long walk.

14. Thrive on attention and let people touch you.

15. Avoid biting when a simple growl will do.

16. On hot days, drink lots of water and lie under a shady tree.

17. When you are happy, dance around and wag your entire body.

18. No matter how often you are criticized, don't buy into the guilt thing and pout. Run right back and make friends.

DoG WiSDOM

Be brave no matter your size.

Take a nap. Hide your favorite snack.

Make your own fun.

Have a mind of your own.

Unleash your talents.

Learn new tricks no matter your age.

Dig life.

Make new friends.

Sniff out opportunities.

Chase after your dreams.

ACKNOWLEDGMENTS

We've made every reasonable effort to locate original sources, obtain permission to use copyright protected content, and supply complete and correct credits. If there are errors or omissions, please contact info@quippery.com so we can address corrections in any subsequent edition.

Twitter
Our heartfelt thanks to all the Twitter users who allowed us to include their great tweets. Please check them all out on Twitter!

Dog silhouettes from www.Vecteezy.com

Where do dogs really *come from?*
© 2018 by Robert Wilde. Reprinted by permission of the author.

Have you ever wondered why people have pets?
Excerpt from BAD HABITS: A 100% FACT FREE BOOK by Dave Barry, copyright © 1987 by Dave Barry. Used by permission of Writers House, LLC. All rights reserved.

Pets Immediately Available for Adoption
"Pets immediately available for adoption," 9/3/2016, Jason Roeder. Jason Roeder/The New Yorker © Conde Nast.

GIVING BACK

We pledge to donate a percentage of our profits in support of planet and people, through the vital work of two nonprofit organizations:

Planet

Since 1951, The Nature Conservancy (www.nature.org) has worked to protect the lands and waters on which all life depends.

People

The David Lynch Foundation (www.davidlynchfoundation.org) supports the health, well-being, and personal development of at-risk students, veterans suffering from PTSD, women and girls who have been the victims of violence, people living with HIV/AIDS, prisoners, and at-risk children in other countries.

MORE FROM QUIPPERY!

If you haven't done so already, please check out:

FUR & PURR
THE FUNNIEST THINGS PEOPLE HAVE SAID ABOUT
CATS

And more Quippery books are on the way. Just go to Quippery.com and sign up on our email list. We'll let you know when they're available.

If there's any way we can improve this book, we'd love to hear from you at feedback@quippery.com.

Finally, we'd be grateful for your review on Amazon. Please go to Amazon.com and search for "Quippery."

THANKS FOR READING!

Made in the USA
Middletown, DE
16 December 2019